Divorce
in North Carolina

Answers to Your Legal Questions

William C. Trosch, Esq.
Eric C. Trosch, Esq.

Addicus Books
Omaha, Nebraska

An Addicus Nonfiction Book

ISBN: 978-1-940495-99-6

Typography Jack Kusler

This book is not intended to serve as a substitute for an attorney. Nor is it the authors' intent to give legal advice contrary to that of an attorney.

Library of Congress Cataloging-in-Publication Data

Names: Trosch, William C., author. | Trosch, Eric C., author.
Title: Divorce in North Carolina : answers to your legal questions / William C. Trosch, Esq., Eric C. Trosch, Esq.
Description: Omaha, Nebraska : Addicus Books, Inc., 2016. | Includes index. | "An Addicus nonfiction book."
Identifiers: LCCN 2016023109 | ISBN 9781943886036 (alk. paper) | ISBN 9781943886500 (Epub) ISBN 9781943886517 (Mobi) | ISBN 9781943886494 (PDF)
Subjects: LCSH: Divorce—Law and legislation—North Carolina—Miscellanea.
Classification: LCC KFN7500 .T76 2016
DDC 346.75601/66—dc23
LC record available at https://lccn.loc.gov/2016023109

Addicus Books, Inc.
P.O. Box 45327
Omaha, Nebraska 68145
www.AddicusBooks.com
Printed in the United States of America
10 9 8 7 6 5 4 3 2 1

Dedication

To Minette Trosch, our mother, mentor, and inspiration. Your perseverance helped shape us into the men we are today. You showed us that challenges are merely opportunities to do our best. For more than forty years you led Charlotte from a quiet town to the Queen City of the New South.

You flew from your empty nest to law school. You started what is now our firm's family law practice. You worked tirelessly as you showed us that the legal profession was about service to the community.

We learned from you that the practice of law is a career in which we should apply tireless effort, not only to the paying clients, but to help those less fortunate. Quite simply, without you this book would not exist.

Contents

Introduction

We wrote this book to help people know what to expect while navigating the legal process of getting a divorce. That is not to say we are advocating fierce litigation in every situation (or even getting a divorce at all). Understanding what happens during a divorce is just one part of evaluating whether to get a divorce. We believe getting a divorce is a last resort, to be entered into only after you have fully explored all of your options. Understand that your goals and family situation are unique. Knowing what to expect is the first step in evaluating the best course of action for you and your family.

Many clients come to us ready to fight like hell. More than a few clients have said "I don't care if I lose everything fighting in the divorce as long as he gets nothing!" These clients are exhausted, frustrated, and feel as though they are out of options. These are normal feelings, but there are costs to this "scorched earth" approach. If you have children, remember that they do not have the option of exchanging their Mom or Dad for a new one. How you and your spouse conduct yourselves during this trying time can go a long way toward minimizing the adverse effects your children will experience from their parents splitting up.

It takes two sides to compromise. Unfortunately, by the time you are considering divorce, communication between you and your spouse may have broken down, if it exists at all, and a settlement may not be possible. Of course, no book can substitute the advice of an experienced attorney, and this book is not intended to take the place of good counsel. Should you find yourself in need of a road map for the tumultuous storm ahead, we hope this book can guide you to calmer waters.

1

Understanding the Divorce Process

Divorce is scary. Life feels out of control. Nothing about the process seems to make sense. Overwhelming anxiety sets in: fear of the pain, the legal process, the cost, the future, and, especially, fear of the unknown. At a time when your life can feel like it is in utter chaos, sometimes the smallest bit of predictability can bring a sense of comfort. There is one part of your divorce that does have some measure of predictability, and that is the divorce process itself.

Most divorces proceed in a step-by-step manner. Despite the uniqueness of your divorce, you can generally count on one phase of your divorce following the next. Sometimes just realizing you are completing stages and moving forward with your divorce can reassure you that it will not go on forever.

It is important to develop a basic understanding of the divorce process. This will lower your anxiety when you feel your heart start pounding in fear while your attorney starts talking about "depositions" or "going to trial." Knowledge can reduce your frustration about the length of the process because you understand why each step is needed. It will help you begin preparing for what comes next.

Most importantly, understanding the divorce process will make your experience of the entire divorce easier. Who wouldn't prefer that?

1.1   What is a *divorce?*

A *divorce* is technically the "dissolution of a marriage." While an absolute divorce results in the dissolution of the legal marriage between the spouses, there are other claims that either must be brought prior to the dissolution of marriage or else be waived, preventing both spouses from ever being allowed to bring those claims. These waivable claims include equitable distribution (dividing up the property and debts) and spousal support (alimony). Other claims that may be relevant to a "divorce" include child custody and child support. For the purposes of this book, we include all these related claims as part of the "divorce," though technically they are separate claims and, in some circumstances (such as child custody and child support), the claims are not even related to a marriage (for instance, if children were born out of wedlock).

1.2   What is my first step?

Find a law firm that handles divorces as a regular part of its law practice. Though a board-certified specialist is not necessary in every case, hiring a firm with a family law division led by a specialist is important. Ask around. The best recommendations come from people who have knowledge of a lawyer's experience and reputation. Go to a law firm's website and look at the qualifications of the lawyer and the firm.

Start planning ahead, even if you are not ready to file for divorce. Call to schedule an appointment right away to obtain information about protecting yourself and your children. You should know your options and rights before you decide whether to proceed with a divorce. Remember that your spouse might already be preparing for a divorce.

When you speak to someone at the law firm you have chosen, ask what documents you should take to your initial consultation. Make a list of your questions to take to your first meeting. Start making plans for how you will pay your attorney to begin working on your case.

1.3   Must I have an attorney to get a divorce in North Carolina?

You are not required to have an attorney to obtain a divorce in North Carolina. A person who proceeds in a legal matter without a lawyer is referred to as being *pro se* (pronounced "pro-say"), meaning "on one's own." If your case involves children, alimony or spousal support, significant property, or debts, you should avoid proceeding on your own. Sometimes problems created early in a case by a *pro se* individual are irreversible. Other times, mistakes made by people proceeding *pro se* can be corrected (to a degree), but at a much greater cost than if a good attorney had been hired much earlier in the case.

The Divorce Process

The divorce process in North Carolina typically involves the following steps.

If both sides wish to settle, negotiate, or come to a collaborative settlement prior to a lawsuit for dissolution of marriage:

- Obtain a referral for an attorney.
- Schedule an appointment with an attorney.
- Prepare questions and gather documents for an initial consultation.
- Meet for an initial consultation with an attorney.
- Determine whether you want to hire the attorney with whom you met.
- Pay the attorney a retainer and sign a retainer agreement.
- Provide requested information and documents to your attorney.
- Take other actions as advised by your attorney, such as opening or closing financial accounts.
- Discuss your goals for settlement negotiations or a collaborative settlement fully with your attorney and follow your attorney's advice.
- Attorney voluntarily exchanges information with your spouse or your spouse's attorney.
- Attend one or more settlement conferences.
- Attorney drafts settlement documents, if the case settles.

If you are initiating the divorce before speaking with your spouse (after speaking with your attorney you may want to postpone or not pursue a divorce):

- Obtain a referral for an attorney.
- Schedule an appointment with an attorney.
- Prepare questions and gather documents for an initial consultation.
- Meet for an initial consultation with an attorney.
- Determine whether you want to hire the attorney with whom you met.
- Pay the attorney a retainer and sign a retainer agreement.
- Provide requested information and documents to your attorney.
- Take other actions as advised by your attorney, such as opening or closing financial accounts.
- Develop a tailored strategy for your individual needs. This strategy may focus on an out-of-court strategy or proceeding with litigation. This step is essential to how quickly, efficiently, and smoothly your case will be resolved.
- Attorney prepares the *summons and complaint* for your review and signature.
- Attorney files the summons and complaint with the clerk of the court.
- Attorney serves the summons and petition on your spouse.
- If interim relief (such as temporary child support, spousal support, or attorney fees) is appropriate, attorney prepares motion papers for your review and signature, files with the court, obtains court date, and serves pleadings on respondent.

If you have been served with divorce papers:

- Obtain a referral for an attorney.
- Schedule an appointment with an attorney.
- Prepare questions and gather necessary documents for an initial consultation.

- Meet for an initial consultation with an attorney.
- Pay the attorney a retainer and sign a retainer agreement.
- Provide requested information and documents to your attorney.
- Take other actions as advised by your attorney, such as opening or closing financial accounts.
- Develop a tailored strategy for your individual needs. This strategy may focus on an out-of-court strategy or proceeding with litigation. This step is essential to how quickly, efficiently, and smoothly your case will be resolved.
- Attorney prepares a response to the summons and petition for your review and signature.
- Attorney files your response with the clerk of the court, usually within thirty days of service of the petition and summons on you.
- If you are served with requests for interim relief, attorney prepares your response to these requests.

After an action has been commenced and the response filed:

- With the assistance of your attorney, you will need to prepare financial disclosure documents (income and expense declaration and preliminary schedule of assets and debts).
- Negotiations begin regarding temporary custody and visitation, child and spousal support, payment of community obligations, and attorney fees.
- Attorney prepares any requests for temporary relief not previously made.
- If there are minor children, the parties comply with any local rules or court orders to attend parent orientation and to participate in mandatory mediation.
- Court holds hearing(s) on request(s) for temporary relief.
- Either the parties reach an agreement or the court issues temporary orders.

- Temporary order is prepared by one attorney, approved as to form by other attorney, and submitted to the judge for signature.
- Both sides conduct *discovery* (the process designed to obtain information regarding all relevant facts), and commence the process to exchange valuations of all assets, including expert opinions if needed.
- You confer with your attorney to review facts, identify issues, assess strengths and weaknesses of case, review strategy, and develop a settlement proposal.
- Spouses, with the support of their attorneys, attempt to reach agreement through written proposals, mediation, settlement conferences, or other forms of negotiation.

If you reach an agreement on all issues, then:
- Your attorney prepares *marital settlement agreement* and necessary paperwork.
- Both parties and their attorneys sign agreement and all necessary paperwork.
- Paperwork may be filed with the court.
- Either the parties waive the court date or the court holds a brief, final hearing.
- Judgment is entered and you will be divorced.
- Your attorney completes necessary orders and supervises the property transfer until all agreed terms are satisfied.

If you are *unable* to reach an agreement on all issues, then:
- Your attorney completes all necessary discovery to bring the case to its trial-ready point.
- Your attorney files an *at-issue memorandum* to obtain trial dates.
- If agreement has been reached on *any* issues, your attorney prepares a *stipulation* on those issues. All other issues are set for trial.
- You work with your attorney to prepare your case for trial.

- Your attorney prepares witnesses, trial exhibits, legal research on contested issues, pretrial motions, trial briefs, direct and cross-examination of witnesses, opening statements, witness subpoenas, and your closing argument.
- You meet with your attorney for final trial preparation.
- Trial is held.
- Your attorney requests a *statement of decision.*
- The judge issues a *tentative statement of decision* and directs the statement to be prepared.
- Both sides make any objections they have to the statement of decision. If appropriate, the court sets the matter for hearing.
- The judge signs the *final statement of decision* and *judgment of dissolution,* dissolving your marriage or domestic partnership.
- The attorneys supervise any property transfers until all agreed terms are satisfied.

Your posttrial rights are discussed in chapter 16 on appeals.

1.4 Should I settle with my spouse first, then get an attorney to "draw up the papers"?

You should not settle anything until you know what you are settling or you will likely base your settlement negotiations on inaccurate or incomplete information. Though the Internet can be a great supplemental resource, you should avoid relying on it for understanding your legal rights. You may see laws from other states which differ from North Carolina's and incorrectly assume the laws are the same. In addition, North Carolina laws themselves change frequently and judges may even differ from county to county (or even within the same county). You may not be able to understand the context of what is being written on the Internet. Finally, and probably most importantly: Even for North Carolina sites, much of what is on the Internet is just simply wrong and it can be difficult to determine which sites provide correct information and which sites do not.

Let's say you do give the "keep lawyers out of it" approach a chance and, armed with all of your (hopefully correct) independent research, you approach your spouse to negotiate a settlement. You make a reasonable offer with the expectation that your spouse will see it like you do. They never do. Once you make offers or concessions to your spouse, it is very difficult (if not impossible) to take them back later. For instance, you may be entitled to alimony and not know it. If you were to tell your spouse that you were not going to seek alimony, your spouse will take that as a given in future negotiations. Yes, you can sometimes legally take back these offers and concessions, but that does not mean that your spouse will be open to giving them back to you in a settlement, driving the case to an inevitable (and expensive) trial.

If you do want to try and settle yourself, it is a wise move to meet with an attorney. Be sure you understand your rights and how to make a negotiation plan so that you do not make your lawyer's job in future negotiations more difficult than it needs to be.

1.5   Is North Carolina a no-fault state or do I need grounds for a divorce?

North Carolina, like most states, is a *no-fault divorce state.* This means that neither you nor your spouse is required to prove that the other is "at fault" in order to be granted a divorce. Though they may be relevant to other domestic law issues, factors such as infidelity, cruelty, or abandonment are not necessary to receive a divorce in North Carolina. Rather, North Carolina allows divorces in two circumstances:

- Separation for at least one year
- Incurable insanity (which is almost never used anymore)

1.6   Do I have to get divorced in the same state I married in?

No. Regardless of where you were married, you may seek a divorce in North Carolina if the jurisdictional requirements of residency are met.

1.7 How long must I have lived in North Carolina to get a divorce in the state?

Either you or your spouse must have been a resident of the State of North Carolina for at least the six months immediately before the divorce proceedings are filed. This is referred to as the *jurisdictional residency requirement* for a divorce in North Carolina.

1.8 My spouse has told me she will never "give me" a divorce. Can I get one in North Carolina anyway?

Yes. North Carolina does not require that your spouse "agree to" a divorce. If your spouse threatens to "not give you a divorce," know that in North Carolina this is likely to be an idle threat without any basis in the law.

1.9 Can I divorce my spouse in North Carolina if he or she lives in another state?

Provided you have met the residency requirements for living in North Carolina for six months, you can file for divorce in North Carolina even if your spouse lives in another state.

Discuss with your attorney the facts that will need to be proven and the steps necessary to give your spouse proper notice to ensure that the court will have jurisdiction over your spouse. Your attorney can counsel you on whether it is possible to proceed with the divorce.

1.10 How can I divorce my spouse when I don't know where my spouse lives now?

North Carolina law allows you to proceed with a divorce even if you do not know the current address of your spouse. This is a very difficult process and is full of procedural land mines. It is one in which a good attorney will be needed (and maybe a good private investigator).

First, take action to attempt to locate your spouse. Contact family members, friends, former coworkers, or anyone else who might know your spouse's whereabouts.

Utilize resources on the Internet that are designed to help locate people.

Let your attorney know of the efforts you have made to attempt to find your spouse. Inform your lawyer of your spouse's last known address, as well as any work address or other address where he or she may be found. Once your attorney attempts to give notice to your spouse without success, it is possible to proceed with the divorce by giving notice through publication in a newspaper.

Although your divorce may be granted following service of notice by publication in a newspaper, it may be more difficult to get other court orders, such as those for child support or alimony, without giving personal notice to your spouse. Talk to your attorney about your options and rights if you do not know where your spouse is living.

1.11 I just moved to a different county. Do I have to file in the county where my spouse lives?

You may file your divorce action either in the county where you reside or the county where your spouse resides. For example, if you live in Charlotte (Mecklenburg County) and your spouse lives in Raleigh (Wake County), you may file your divorce action in either Mecklenburg County or Wake County.

1.12 I really need a divorce quickly. Will the divorce I get in another state or country be valid in North Carolina?

If both you and your spouse regard North Carolina as your true home and you both intend to remain in the state, a divorce from another state or country will not be valid. If North Carolina is the permanent home for both of you, you cannot obtain a valid divorce in another state or country, even if you reside there temporarily.

1.13 I immigrated to North Carolina. Will my immigration status stop me from getting a divorce?

If you meet the residency requirements for divorce in North Carolina, you can get a divorce here regardless of your immigration status. Talk to your immigration lawyer about the likelihood of a divorce leading to immigration challenges.

If you are a victim of domestic violence, tell your lawyer. You may be eligible for a change in your immigration status under the federal *Violence Against Women Act.*

1.14 How long after the divorce is started can I actually get the divorce?

In North Carolina, it depends greatly from county to county. After the *defendant* (the spouse who did not start the proceedings) is "served" (has been given legal notice of the divorce), the spouse has at least thirty days to respond. This date is either the day that the defendant is personally delivered papers in a legally authorized manner—for example, the papers may be delivered by a sheriff or by certified mail—or, it may be the date that the defendant files a *voluntary appearance notice,* acknowledging that he or she knows the divorce has been filed with the court.

Your spouse can delay the proceedings by asking for an additional thirty days to answer your divorce allegations. After the time to answer the allegations has passed, you can have a hearing thirteen days after you provide notice of the hearing to your spouse. So, without your spouse trying to delay the process, it will take at least one and one-half months to get your divorce. A better estimate would be three to four months to get your divorce.

Do not forget that there are other issues, such as custody, support, property, and debts, that may need to be resolved. These other issues can be resolved before or after the divorce, so long as you file for these claims prior to the entry of the divorce.

1.15 What is a *divorce complaint?*

A *divorce complaint* is a document signed by the person filing for divorce. It is filed with the clerk of the court to initiate the divorce process. The complaint will present in very general terms what the plaintiff is asking the court to order; it may include all of the issues the person filing for divorce wants the court to rule on (things such as alimony, equitable distribution, child custody, and child support).

1.16 My spouse said she filed for divorce last week, but my lawyer says there's nothing on file at the courthouse. What does it mean to "file for divorce?"

When a lawsuit is initiated, the court will create a paper "file" that will hold the court documents for your lawsuit. Your file will be given a file number and in many counties you will be assigned a judge. Thereafter, technically, a lawyer "files" a legal document at the courthouse by presenting it to the clerk of court so that she can place the document in the court's file. The clerk of court will "file stamp" (print the date and time onto the document that was presented to the court) the document. The clerk of court also will "file stamp" copies of the document for the lawyer to keep for his or her file to prove the document was actually filed.

To "file for divorce" is to simply start the legal proceedings at the courthouse by "filing" the first papers of the divorce and having the clerk of court set up a court file for the divorce case. Sometimes a person who has hired a lawyer to begin a divorce action uses the phrase, "I've filed for divorce," meaning that they have started the process by getting an attorney, even though the attorney has not yet taken any papers to the courthouse to officially start the legal process.

1.17   If we both want a divorce, does it matter who files?

It depends. In the eyes of the court, the *plaintiff* (the spouse who files the complaint initiating the divorce) and the *defendant* (the other spouse) are not seen differently by virtue of which party filed. Oftentimes in divorce actions, lawyers and judges dispense with the formal titles of plaintiff and defendant when discussing the case and use *husband* and *wife* or *father* and *mother.*

That said, your attorney may advise you to file first or to wait until your spouse files, depending upon the overall strategy for your case and your circumstances. For example, if you are separated from your spouse but have a beneficial temporary arrangement, your attorney may counsel you to wait for your spouse to file. On the other hand, if your children live with your spouse, you may want to institute the legal process to allow you to have custody of, or more visitation with, your children sooner than if you waited for your spouse to file first.

Allow your attorney to support you in making the decision about when to initiate the legal process by filing a complaint.

1.18 Can I stop the newspaper from publishing notice of the filing or granting of my divorce?

Documents filed with the court, such as a divorce complaint, are a matter of public record. Newspapers have a right to access this information, and many newspapers publish this information as a matter of routine. Newspapers that publish such notices typically do so within a week of the date that documents are filed with the clerk of the court.

In very rare cases, a divorce file (or portions of it) may be kept private, referred to as being "sealed" or "under seal" if the court orders it. In North Carolina it is very difficult to keep a document confidential if it is filed with the court. The rights of the public to access court documents is very broad in North Carolina. That being said, it is not very convenient to access court files. Typically, there is not much information available online about one's divorce case. It would take someone a lot of effort to get that kind of information. If you desire to keep the details of your divorce private, you may want to pursue a confidential collaborative law solution or attempt to resolve your dispute through binding arbitration, either of which would keep the record from becoming public and this would allow you greater control over the confidentiality of the proceedings.

1.19 Is there a way to avoid embarrassing my spouse and not have the sheriff serve him or her with the divorce papers at the workplace?

The sheriff is only one of the ways that you may serve your spouse with the divorce papers. The easiest way to obtain service would be to have your spouse sign a document known as an *acceptance of service* (talk to your lawyer about preparing this document). Other options may include delivery by certified mail, a designated delivery service (such as Fed Ex or UPS), or a private *process server,* an individual that hands the papers to your spouse. Of course, if your spouse refuses to sign for or accept the documents, the best option may end up being the sheriff, but you would have given your spouse the chance to avoid embarrassment by accepting service through another method.

1.20 Should I sign an *acceptance of service* even if I don't agree with what my spouse has written in the complaint for divorce?

In most cases, signing the *acceptance of service* does not mean that you agree with anything your spouse has stated in the divorce complaint or anything that your spouse is asking for in the divorce. Signing the acceptance of service should only substitute for having the sheriff personally hand you the documents. It is, however, important to read what is actually written in the acceptance of service and, preferably, review it with your attorney so that you are not waiving any of your rights.

With a properly drafted acceptance of service, you should not waive the right to object to anything your spouse has stated in the complaint. Accepting service will initiate the legal process. With that, court deadlines will begin to move forward. It is essential to follow your attorney's advice on whether and when to sign an acceptance of service.

1.21 Why should I contact an attorney right away if I have received divorce papers?

Procrastinating on responding to served divorce papers can cause irreparable damage to your case. There are deadlines to respond to the complaint (typically thirty days). Missing these deadlines can cause you to lose your case. Of course, you must also take into account the practicalities of hiring a lawyer to help you formulate a defense and prepare an *answer* to the complaint. Many times, appointments with attorneys are not immediately available. Furthermore, your attorney will need time to prepare and file your written answer properly. If you wait until a few days before your deadline, you may be preparing your answer alone (with potentially disastrous results).

If your spouse has filed for divorce, it is important that you obtain legal advice as soon as possible. Even if you and your spouse are getting along, having independent legal counsel can help you make decisions now that could affect your divorce later.

Sometimes there are temporary issues that pop up quickly in a case. It is possible you will receive only a few days' notice of a temporary hearing. This hearing is a court proceeding, usually at the beginning of the case, in which the judge decides what arrangements will be made with the divorcing couple while their case is under way. The hearing can determine such things as establishing temporary custody or a visitation schedule, allowing for temporary support for one of the spouses, setting up child-support payments, and keeping the couple from using marital assets. You will be better prepared for a temporary hearing if you have already retained an attorney.

1.22   What is an *ex parte court order?*

An *ex parte court order* is obtained by one party going to the judge to ask for something without giving prior notice or an opportunity to be heard by the other side.

Judges often are reluctant to sign *ex parte* orders. Ordinarily the court will require the other side to have notice of any requests for court orders, and a hearing before the judge will be held.

An *affidavit,* which is a written statement sworn under oath, is usually required before a judge will sign an *ex parte* order. *Ex parte* orders are generally limited to emergency situations such as requests for emergency custody, temporary restraining orders, and domestic violence protection orders.

When an *ex parte* order is granted, the party who did not request the order will have an opportunity to have a subsequent hearing before the judge to determine whether the order should remain in effect. Typically, these "return hearings" are scheduled within a few weeks and the hearings often have time limits. That is why it is important to get legal counsel involved early to protect your rights.

1.23   What is a *motion?*

When your attorney asks the judge to order something, it typically is called a *motion.* There are *procedural motions* and there are *substantive motions.* Many motions are made to handle certain procedural aspects of your case, such as a motion for extension of time asking that the court extend a deadline. These procedural motions are important, but usually not critical to your case. In fact, many of the procedural motions are consented to by both sides as a matter of professional courtesy or to save money (why fight in court when you know how the judge is likely to rule?).

Other motions are more substantive and deserve more attention. These types of motions are more typically litigated in a court hearing. For example, your attorney may file a written motion with the court asking for temporary child custody and temporary child support. The result of this motion may set a precedent for the rest of the case, making it critically important.

Motions do not always have to be in writing. In some cases, a motion may be made orally rather than in writing, such as when an issue arises during the course of a court hearing or trial. It is best practice to make most motions in writing as there are limits as to what motions can be done orally.

1.24 After my complaint for divorce is filed, how long will it take before a temporary hearing is held to decide what happens with our child and our finances while the divorce is pending?

This varies from county to county so it is a good idea to check with the local rules of your particular court for specifics. In most counties, if there are grounds for a temporary hearing and available court time, these urgent issues are often heard within a month or two from the filing of the motion for temporary relief.

1.25 How much notice will I get if my spouse seeks a temporary order?

This varies greatly from county to county so it is a good idea to check with the local rules of your particular court for specifics. North Carolina law does allow for shortened periods of notice for motions for temporary orders; accordingly, this notice may be as short as a few days.

1.26 During my divorce, what am I responsible for doing?

Your attorney will explain what actions you should take to further the divorce process and to help you reach the best possible outcome.

You will be asked to:

- Keep the clerk of court notified of all of your current contact information and/or your attorney's contact information.
- Develop and convey your goals to your attorney.
- Keep in regular contact with your attorney.
- Update your attorney regarding any changes in your contact information, such as address, phone numbers, and e-mail address.
- Provide your attorney with all requested documents.
- Provide requested information in a timely manner.
- Complete forms and questionnaires.
- Appear in court on time.
- Be direct about asking any questions you might have.
- Tell your attorney your thoughts on settlement or what you would like the judge to order in your case.
- Remain respectful toward your spouse throughout the process.
- Comply with any temporary court orders, such as restraining or support orders.
- Advise your attorney of any significant developments in your case.
- Be careful about your usage of social media.

By doing your part in the divorce process, you enable your attorney to partner with you for a better outcome while also lowering your attorney fees.

1.27 I'm worried that I won't remember to ask my lawyer about all of the issues in my case. How can I be sure I don't miss anything?

Write down all of the topics you want to discuss with your attorney, including what your goals are for the outcome of the divorce. The sooner you have clear goals, the easier it will be for your attorney to support you in getting what you want. Realize that your attorney will think of some issues that you may not have considered. Your lawyer's experience will be helpful in making sure nothing important is forgotten. Use the Divorce Issues Checklist on the following pages as a guide.

Divorce Issues Checklist

Issue	Notes
Dissolution of marriage—divorce	
Temporary custody of minor children	
Permanent custody of minor children	
Removal of children from jurisdiction	
Parenting Plan (time, transportation)	
Temporary child support	
Permanent child support	
Extraordinary expenses warranting a deviation in child support	
Summer child-care costs	
Life insurance or a qualified domestic relations order (QDRO) to fund unpaid child support	
Imputing income for child-support purposes	
Child-support arrears and collection	
Automatic withholding for support	
After-school and other work-related child-care expenses	
Health insurance on minor children and qualified medical child-support orders (QMCSOs)	
Uninsured medical expenses for minor children	
Private school tuition for children	
College expenses for children	
Health insurance on the parties	
Real property: marital residence (deed, refinancing, sale)	
Real property: rentals, cabins, commercial property (deed, refinancing, sale)	
Marital expenses associated with real estate	

Divorce Issues Checklist (Continued)

Issue	Notes
Time-shares	
Retirement plans (401k, Simple IRA, TSA, pensions), possible qualified domestic relations orders (QDRO)	
Pensions (private, government, military)	
Survivor benefits (pensions—private, government, military)	
Thrift savings plan	
Businesses	
Bank accounts	
Investments	
Stock options	
Premarital or nonmarital assets	
Premaritial or nonmarital debts	
Pets	
Personal property division: including motor vehicles, recreational vehicles, campers, airplanes, collections, furniture, electronics, tools, household goods	
Exchange date for personal property	
Country club memberships, seat licenses, frequent-flyer miles	
Division of marital debt	
Property settlement	
Alimony (your needs, your spouse's individual needs and expenses)	
Life insurance to fund unpaid alimony	
Sums owed under temporary order	
Tax exemptions for minor children	

Divorce Issues Checklist (Continued)

Issue	Notes
IRS Form 8332 for claiming children as dependents	
Filing status for tax returns for last/current year	
Restoration of former name	
Attorney fees	

1.28 My spouse has all of our financial information. How will I be able to prepare for negotiations and trial if I don't know the facts or have the documents?

Ideally, your spouse and you will be able to save money by voluntarily exchanging necessary financial information to assist in the settlement of your case. Once your divorce has been filed with court and temporary matters have been addressed, your attorney can also proceed with a process known as *discovery*. Through discovery, your attorney can formally ask your spouse to provide documents and information needed to prepare your case. (We will cover discovery in more detail in chapter 5).

1.29 My spouse and I both want our divorce to be amicable. How can we keep it that way?

Find a lawyer who understands your goal to reach settlement and encourage your spouse to do the same. Consider choosing a lawyer that understands and has experience with *collaborative law* (a process that attempts to settle cases amicably and outside the adversarial court system).

Once you start the process, cooperate in the prompt voluntary exchange of necessary information. Then, ask your attorney about the options of negotiation and mediation for reaching an agreement. Even if you are not able to settle all of the issues in your divorce, these actions can increase the likelihood of agreement on many issues that would otherwise be taken to court.

You and your spouse should be commended for your willingness to cooperate while focusing on moving through the divorce process. This will not only make your lives easier and save you money on attorney fees, but it is also more likely to result in an outcome you are both satisfied with. In addition, collaborative law proceedings can reduce stress on the children by keeping them from being exposed (directly or indirectly) to the adversarial litigation process.

1.30   Can I get a different judge?

In North Carolina many judicial districts are run by a *family court administrator*. In these jurisdictions, you may be assigned a judge for the duration of your case. In smaller districts, many different judges may handle your case. Talk to your attorney about the reasons you want a different judge. If you believe that your judge has a conflict of interest, such as being a close friend with your spouse, you may have a basis for asking the judge to be "recused" in order to allow another judge to hear the case. So, in simple terms, you cannot pick your own judge. A judge may not be able to hear your case if he or she has a conflict of interest.

1.31   What is the significance of my divorce being final?

The finality of your divorce decree is important for many reasons. It can affect your right to remarry, your estate rights, your eligibility for health insurance from your former spouse, and your filing status for income taxes. In addition, when a divorce becomes final, it can terminate the ability for either spouse to assert certain claims (if they have not already been made), such as asking the court to equitably divide the marital property or grant spousal support.

1.32   When does my divorce become final?

Usually, after the judge signs your divorce decree, your divorce is final, but if your spouse does not receive the decree in court, it is not effective until the decree has been served on both spouses. Again, the issues related to divorce (property, custody, support, and property division) are not always resolved on this date. Those issues may be resolved before or after the divorce decree, depending on when they are filed. The sooner these items are filed the quicker they will be resolved.

**1.33   Can I start using my former name right away and how
do I get my name legally restored?**

You may begin using your former name at any time, provided you are not doing so for any unlawful purpose, such as
avoiding your creditors. Many agencies and institutions, however, will not alter their records without a court order changing
your name.

If you want your former name restored, let your attorney
know so that this provision can be included in your divorce
decree. If you want to change your legal name after the divorce and have not provided for it in your divorce decree, it
may be necessary for you to undergo a separate legal action
for a name change.

2

Coping with Stress
during the Divorce Process

Coping with a divorce can be extremely stressful. Whether you have been married for a few years or a few decades, working through the emotions between "I do" and "I don't" can leave you feeling overwhelmed, exhausted, and unable to manage the changes you are going through. Many aspects of your divorce may leave you feeling left out and filled with doubts. What will my family think? Am I a failure? Am I making the right decision for my children?

A wide range of emotions is par for the course. You may feel angry, depressed, sad, indifferent, or relieved throughout the process. Whatever you are feeling, know that you are not alone. During this volatile time, it is important to remember you have family and friends with whom to share your worries. Reaching out to your support system is crucial when you are facing a divorce.

Knowing the process and what to expect may also help reduce your stress. Express your feelings to your support system and let the goals you have set guide you through the process.

2.1   My spouse left home weeks ago. I don't want a divorce because I feel our marriage can be saved. Should I still see an attorney?

It's a good idea to see an attorney. Whether you want a divorce or not, there may be important actions for you to take now to protect your assets, credit, home, children, and future right to support. A good attorney will work with you to help you find the right professionals to help you save your marriage.

It is best to be prepared with the support of an attorney, even if you decide not to file for a divorce at this time. If your spouse files for divorce, a temporary hearing could be held in just a matter of days.

2.2 The thought of going to a lawyer's office to talk about divorce is more than I can bear. I canceled the first appointment I made because I just couldn't do it. What should I do?

Many people going through a divorce are dealing with lawyers for the first time and feel anxious about the experience. Ask a trusted friend or family member to go with you. While you will want to speak with the attorney by yourself when confidential topics arise (for your and your friend's protection), most lawyers are happy to go over the laws of North Carolina and general principles with someone else present. It is very likely that you will feel greatly relieved just to be better informed.

2.3 There is some information about my marriage that I think my attorney needs, but I'm too embarrassed to discuss it. Must I tell the attorney?

Yes. Although it may feel uncomfortable, it is important that you provide your attorney with complete information so that your interests can be fully protected. If speaking directly about these facts still seems too hard, consider putting them in a letter.

Attorneys who practice divorce law are accustomed to hearing a lot of intimate information about families. Even though it is deeply personal to you, it is unlikely that anything you tell your lawyer will be shocking to him or her. It is much better for you to tell your attorney this information early on, rather than for your attorney to find out about it later in the case. By then, your attorney is less able to plan for the "surprise" information quickly during a court hearing. Most issues can be "fixed" or at least improved if an attorney is given enough lead time to develop a strategy.

Your attorney has an ethical duty to maintain confidentiality. Past events in your marriage are matters that your lawyer is obligated to keep private. The reason for this ethical duty is so that attorney's clients can be more comfortable in sharing all relevant information so the lawyer can better represent them.

2.4   I'm unsure about how to tell our children about the divorce, and I'm worried I'll say the wrong thing. What's the best way?

How you talk to your children about the divorce will depend upon their ages and development. Changes in your children's everyday lives, such as a change of residence or one parent leaving the home, are far more important to them than the details about the legal proceedings. Information about legal proceedings and meetings with lawyers are best kept among adults.

Simpler answers are best for young children. Avoid giving them more information than they need and whatever you do, do not talk badly about the other parent to your children. Use the adults in your life as a source of support to meet your own emotional needs.

After the initial discussion, keep the door open to further talks by creating opportunities for your children to talk about the divorce. Use these times to acknowledge their feelings and offer support. Always assure them that the divorce is not their fault and that they are still loved by both you and your spouse, regardless of the divorce.

2.5   My youngest child seems very depressed about our divorce, the middle one is angry, and my teenager is skipping school. How can I cope?

A child's reaction to divorce can vary depending upon his or her age and other factors. Some may cry and beg for a reconciliation, and others may act out. Reducing conflict with your spouse, being a consistent and nurturing parent, and making sure both of you remain involved with your children are all actions that can support your children regardless of how they are reacting to the divorce.

Support groups for children whose parents are divorcing are also available at many schools and religious communities. A school counselor can also provide support. If more help is needed, confer with a therapist experienced in working with children.

2.6 **I am so frustrated by my spouse always trying to look like the "favorite" parent, leaving me to be seen as the parent who disciplines the children. Is there anything I can do to stop this?**

Feelings of guilt, competition, or remorse sometimes lead a parent to be tempted to spend parenting time on trips to the toy store and special activities. Other times they can result in an absence of discipline in an effort to become the favored parent or to make the time "special." This is not unusual and the courts usually refrain from intervention in these circumstances.

Shift your focus from the other parent's actions to your own, and do your best to be an outstanding parent during this time. This includes keeping a routine for your child for family meals, bedtimes, chores, and homework. Encourage family activities, as well as individual time with each child when it's possible.

During a time when your child's life is changing, providing a consistent and stable routine in your home can ease your child's anxiety and provide comfort.

2.7 **Between requests for information from my spouse's lawyer and my own lawyer, I am totally overwhelmed. How do I manage gathering all of this detailed information by the deadlines imposed?**

First, simply get started. Often the thought about a task is worse than the job itself. Making a list to organize the information can help keep you from being overwhelmed and ensure you do not forget anything that is being asked of you.

Second, break it down into smaller tasks. Perhaps one evening you gather your tax returns and on the weekend you work on your monthly living expenses.

Third, let in support. Ask that friend of yours who just loves numbers to come over for an evening with her calculator to help you get organized.

Finally, communicate with your lawyer. Your attorney or paralegal may be able to make your job easier by giving you suggestions or help. It may be that essential information can be provided now and the details submitted later.

2.8   I am so depressed about my divorce that I'm having difficulty getting out of bed in the morning to care for my children. What should I do?

See your health care provider. Feelings of depression are common during a divorce. You also want to make sure that you identify any physical health concerns.

Although feelings of sadness and anxiety are common during a divorce, more serious depression means it's time to seek professional support. Sometimes speaking with a trained professional about your feelings during this difficult time can help you cope with stress and feelings of depression.

Your health and your ability to care for your children are essential. Follow through on recommendations by your health care professionals for therapy, medication, or other measures to improve your wellness.

2.9   I know I need help to cope with the stress of the divorce, but I can't afford counseling. What can I do?

You are wise to recognize that divorce is a time for letting in support. You can explore a number of options, including:

- Meeting with a member of the clergy or lay chaplain
- Joining a divorce support group; which may offer tremendous support
- Turning to friends and family members
- Going to a therapist or divorce coach. If budget is a concern, contact a social agency that offers counseling services on a sliding-fee scale.

If none of these options are available, look again at your budget. You may see that counseling is important enough that you decide to find a way to increase your income or lower your expenses to support this investment in your well-being.

2.10   I'm the one who filed for divorce, but I still have loving feelings toward my spouse and feel sad about divorcing. Does this mean I should dismiss my divorce?

Not necessarily. Strong feelings of caring about your spouse often persist after a divorce is filed. Whether or not to proceed with a divorce is a deeply personal decision. While feelings can inform us of our thoughts, sometimes they can also cause us to not look at everything there is to see in our situation. Logically weigh what is best for you, considering all of your feelings as well as the facts of the past and your assessment as to what will happen in the future.

Have you and your spouse participated in marriage counseling? Has your spouse refused to seek treatment for an addiction? Are you worried about the safety of you or your children if you remain in the marriage? Can you envision yourself as financially secure if you remain in this marriage? Is your spouse involved in another relationship?

The answer to these questions can help you clear your mind and make a decision about whether to consider reconciliation. Talk to your therapist, coach, or spiritual advisor to help determine the right path for you.

You also may decide to stop or slow the proceedings through a *collaborative law stay*. This can allow you to work toward a resolution of your case outside of court and to bring in neutral experts to assist you and your spouse toward resolving your issues in a more private setting. You should weigh the pros and cons of this option with your attorney.

2.11 Will my lawyer charge me for the time I spend talking about my feelings about my spouse and my divorce?

It depends. If you are paying your attorney by the hour, expect to be charged for the time your attorney spends talking with you. If your attorney is being paid a flat (or possibly a contingent) rate for handling your divorce, the time spent talking with you may be included in the fee.

2.12 My lawyer doesn't seem to realize how difficult my divorce is for me. How can I get my lawyer to understand?

Everyone wants support and compassion from the professionals who are helping them during a divorce. Speak frankly with your attorney about your concerns. It may be that your lawyer does not see your concerns as being relevant to the job of getting your desired outcome in the divorce. Your willingness to improve the communication will help your lawyer understand how best to support you in the process and will help you understand which matters are best left for discussion with your therapist or a supportive friend.

2.13   I've been told not to speak ill of my spouse in front of my child, but I know my spouse is doing this all the time. Why can't I just speak the truth?

It can be devastating for your child to hear you bad-mouthing the other parent. What your child needs is permission to love both of you, regardless of any bad parental behavior. The best way to support your child during this time is to encourage a positive relationship with the other parent. Not only is this the best thing to do for your child psychologically and emotionally, but it typically is the best thing to do for your custody case. Judges do not like it when a parent tries to alienate a child from the other parent.

2.14   Nobody in our family has ever been divorced, and I feel really ashamed. Will my children feel the same way?

Probably, but you can help ameliorate those feelings. Making a change in how you see your family identity is a big challenge. The best way to help your children is to establish a sense of pride in their new family and to look forward to the future with a real sense of potential.

Your children will have an opportunity to witness you overcoming obstacles, demonstrating independence, and moving forward in your life in spite of challenges. You can be a great teacher to them during this time by demonstrating pride in your family and in yourself. Resolving the conflicts of your separation in a healthy and productive way is an important way to help your child grow through this process.

2.15   I am terrified of having my deposition taken. My spouse's lawyer is very aggressive, and I'm afraid I'm going to say something that will hurt my case.

A deposition is an opportunity for your spouse's attorney to gather information and to assess the type of witness you will be if the case proceeds to trial. Feeling anxious about your deposition is normal. However, regardless of the personality of the lawyers, most depositions in divorces are quite uneventful.

Remember that your attorney will be seated by your side at all times to support you. It is natural to fear the unknown, so ask to meet with your lawyer in advance to prepare for the deposition. If you are worried about certain questions that might be asked, talk to your attorney about them. Think of a deposition as an opportunity to tell your story, and enlist your lawyer's support in being well prepared.

2.16   I am still so angry at my spouse. How can I be expected to sit in the same room during a settlement conference?

If you are still really angry at your spouse, it may be beneficial to postpone the conference for a time. You might also consider seeking some counseling to support you in coping with your feelings of anger.

Another option might be "shuttle" negotiations. With this method, you and your attorney remain in one room while your spouse and his or her attorney are in another. Settlement offers are then relayed between the attorneys throughout the negotiation process by a mediator or through your attorneys. By shifting your focus from your angry feelings to your goal of a settlement, it may be easier to proceed through the process.

2.17   I'm afraid I can't make it through court without having an emotional breakdown. How do I prepare?

A divorce trial can be a highly emotional time, calling for lots of support. Some of these ideas may help you through the process:

- Meet with your lawyer or the firm's staff in advance of your court date to prepare you for court.
- Ask your lawyer whether there are any documents you should review in preparation for court, such as your deposition.
- Visit the courtroom in advance to get comfortable with the surroundings.
- Ask your lawyer about having a family member or friend with you on your court date.
- Ask yourself what the worst thing is that could happen and consider what options you would have if it did.
- Avoid alcohol, eat healthfully, exercise, and have plenty of rest during the period of time leading up to

the court date. Each of these will help you to prepare for the emotions of the day.

- Plan what you intend to wear in advance. Small preparations will lower your stress.

- Visualize the experience going well. Picture yourself sitting in the witness chair, giving clear, confident, and truthful answers to easy questions.

- Arrive early at the courthouse and make sure you have a plan for parking your car if you are not familiar with the area.

- Take slow, deep breaths. Breathing deeply will steady your voice, calm your nerves, and improve your focus.

Your attorney will be prepared to support you throughout the proceedings. By taking the above steps, you can minimize stress and make the experience easier.

2.18   I am really confused. One day I think I've made a mistake, the next day I know I can't go back, and a few minutes later I can hardly wait to be single again. Some days I just don't believe I'm getting divorced. What's happening?

What you are experiencing is normal for a person going through divorce. Denial, transition, and acceptance are common passages for a person going through a divorce. One moment you might feel excited about your future and a few hours later you think your life is ruined.

What can be helpful to remember is that you may not pass from one stage to the next in a direct line. Feelings of anger or sadness may well up in you long after you thought you had moved on. Similarly, your mood might feel bright one day as you may think about your future plans, even though you still miss your spouse.

Taking good care of yourself is essential during this period of your life. What you are going through requires a tremendous amount of energy. Allow yourself to experience your emotions, but also continue moving forward with your life. These steps will help your life get easier day by day.

3

Working with an Attorney

A little knowledge is a dangerous thing. Most people have well-intentioned neighbors, cousins, and complete strangers give advice based on their divorce or what happened to their sister who got divorced in Alaska. If there is only one thing you can be sure of in your divorce, it's that you will be given plenty of advice. Many will insist they know what you should do, even though they haven't the vaguest notion of the facts of your case or the law in North Carolina.

Other times, people close to you will "support" you by telling you what they think you want to hear rather than what you need to hear. "The judge surely will give you sole custody and give your ex visitation one day a month, because it is obvious you are the better parent and your ex is a jerk." This type of comment may validate your feelings, but it also may push you to poor decisions by fanning your emotions instead of carefully weighing the real risks of litigation. The outcomes of trials are notoriously hard to predict; the judge may decide to give your ex primary custody. Beware of guidance advice from these benevolent armchair quarterbacks.

A carefully chosen attorney can be the one person whose advice will matter to you. Your lawyer should be your trusted and supportive advocate at all times throughout your divorce. The counsel of your attorney can affect your life for years to come. You will never regret taking the time and energy to choose the right one for you.

See your relationship with your attorney as a partnership for pursuing what is most important to you. With clear and open attorney-client communication, you'll have the best outcome possible and your entire divorce will be less stressful. By working closely with the right lawyer, you can trust the professional advice you receive and simply thank your cousin Millie for sharing.

3.1 Where do I begin looking for an attorney for my divorce?

There are many ways to find a divorce lawyer. Ask people you trust—friends and family members who have gone through a divorce—if they thought they had a great lawyer (or if their former spouse did). If you know professionals who work with attorneys, ask for a referral to an attorney who is experienced in family law and primarily practices in family law. It is a good idea to hire a law firm that has a North Carolina board-certified family law specialist leading the family law team. The North Carolina State Bar (www.nclawspecialists.gov) lists all of the attorneys who have passed the family law specialist exam and are specialists in your area at. These attorneys have a minimum of five years of experience primarily in family law, have passed lengthy family specialist exams, and have been vetted by other experienced family law professionals.

Consult your local bar association to find out whether they have a referral service. Be sure to specify that you are looking for an attorney who primarily handles divorces or family law cases.

Search online. Many attorneys have websites that provide information about their practice areas, professional associations, experience, and philosophy. Make sure that your attorney and law firm have values that are consistent with yours.

3.2 How do I choose the right attorney?

Choosing the right attorney for your divorce is an important decision. Your attorney should be a trusted professional with whom you feel comfortable sharing information openly. He or she should be a person you can trust and a zealous advocate for your interests.

You will rely upon your attorney to help you make many decisions throughout the course of your divorce. You will also entrust your legal counsel to make a range of strategic and procedural decisions on your behalf.

Consultation for a divorce might be your first meeting with a lawyer. Know that attorneys want to be supportive and to fully inform you. Feel free to seek all of the information you need to help you feel secure in knowing you have made the right choice.

Find an attorney who practices primarily in the family law area. While many attorneys do divorces, it is likely you will have more effective representation at a lower cost from an attorney who already knows the fundamentals of divorce law in North Carolina.

Determine the level of experience you want in your attorney. For example, if you have a short marriage with no children and few assets, an attorney with lesser experience might be a good value for your legal needs. However, if you are anticipating a custody dispute or have complex or substantial assets, a more experienced attorney or family law specialist may better meet your needs.

Consider the qualities in an attorney that are important to you. Even the most experienced and skilled attorney is not right for every client. Ask yourself what it is that you are really looking for in an attorney so you can make your choice with these standards in mind. Make sure your attorney can use all of the tools in the toolbox and knows when to use them.

It is important that you are confident in the attorney you hire. If you are unsure about whether the lawyer is really listening to you or understanding your concerns, keep looking until you find one who will. Your divorce is an important matter. It's critical that you have a professional you can trust.

3.3   Should I interview more than one attorney?

Be willing to interview more than one attorney. Every lawyer has different strengths, and it is important that you find the one that is right for you. Sometimes it is only by meeting with more than one attorney that you see clearly who will best be able to help you reach your goals in the way you want.

Changing lawyers in the middle of litigation can be stressful and costly. It is wise to invest energy at the outset in making the right choice for you.

3.4 My spouse says because we're still friends we should use the same attorney for the divorce. Is this a good idea?

No. Even the most amicable of divorcing couples usually have differing interests. For this reason, it is never recommended that an attorney represent both parties to a divorce. An attorney in North Carolina is ethically prohibited from representing two people with conflicting interests who are in dispute.

Sometimes couples have reached agreements without understanding all of their rights under the law. A client often will benefit from receiving further legal advice on matters such as tax considerations, retirement, and health insurance issues.

It is not uncommon for one party to retain an attorney and for the other party to not do so. In such cases, the party with the attorney files the complaint, and prepares the agreements reached between the parties. The documents are typically sent to the unrepresented spouse for approval. If your spouse has filed for divorce and said that you do not need an attorney, you should nevertheless meet with a lawyer for advice on how proceeding without a lawyer could affect your legal rights.

3.5 What information should I take with me to the first meeting with my attorney?

Attorneys differ on the amount of information they like to see at an initial consultation. If a court proceeding, either a divorce or a protection order, has already been initiated by either you or your spouse, it is important to bring copies of any court documents.

If you have a prenuptial or postnuptial agreement with your spouse, that is another important document for you to bring at the outset of your case.

If you intend to ask for support, either for yourself or for your children, documents evidencing income of both you and your spouse will also be useful. These might include:

- Recent pay stubs
- Individual and business tax returns, W-2s, and 1099s
- Bank statements showing deposits

A statement of your monthly expenses is also helpful.

If your situation is urgent or you do not have access to these documents, do not let it stop you from scheduling your appointment with an attorney. Prompt legal advice about your rights is often more important than having detailed financial information in the beginning. Your attorney can explain to you the options for obtaining these financial records if they are not readily available to you.

Your attorney may ask you to complete a questionnaire at the time of your first meeting. Ask whether it is possible to complete this in advance of your meeting. This can allow you to provide more complete information and to make the most of your appointment time with the lawyer.

3.6 What unfamiliar words might an attorney use at the first meeting?

Law has a language all its own, and attorneys sometimes lapse into "legalese," forgetting that nonlawyers may not recognize words used daily in the practice of law. Some words and phrases you might hear include:

- *Dissolution of marriage*—the divorce
- *Plaintiff*—the person who files the divorce complaint
- *Defendant*—the spouse or other parent who did not file the divorce complaint
- *Jurisdiction*—the authority of a court to make rulings affecting a party
- *Service*—the process of notifying a party about a legal filing
- *Discovery*—the process during which each side provides information to the other
- *Decree*—the final order entered in a divorce
- *Date of separation*—the day when you and your spouse begin to live in separate houses and at least one of you intends it to be permanent

Never hesitate to ask your attorney the meaning of a term. Your complete understanding of your lawyer's advice is essential for you to partner with your advocate as effectively as possible.

3.7 What can I expect at an initial consultation with an attorney?

Most attorneys will ask that you complete a questionnaire prior to the meeting. With very few exceptions, attorneys are required to keep confidential all information you provide.

The nature of the advice you get from an attorney in an initial consultation will depend upon whether you are still deciding whether you want a divorce, whether you are planning for a possible divorce in the future, or whether you are ready to file for divorce right away.

During the meeting, you will have an opportunity to provide the following information to the attorney:

- A brief history of the marriage
- Background information regarding yourself, your spouse, and your children
- Your immediate situation
- Your intentions and goals regarding your relationship with your spouse
- What information you are seeking from the attorney during the consultation

You can expect the attorney to provide the following information to you:

- The procedure for divorce in North Carolina
- The claims related to your separation and how the law treats these issues
- A preliminary list of the issues important in your case
- A preliminary assessment of your rights and responsibilities under the law
- Background information regarding the firm
- Information about fees and billing

While some questions may be impossible for the attorney to answer at the initial consultation because additional information or research is needed, the initial consultation is an opportunity for you to ask all of the questions you have at the time of the meeting.

3.8 Can I take a friend or family member to my initial consultation?

Yes. Having someone present during your initial consultation can be a source of great support. Your friend or family member may be able to take notes on your behalf so that you can focus on listening to your attorney and asking questions.

Remember that this is your consultation and it is important that the attorney hear the facts of your case directly from you. To preserve the confidentiality of what is said between you and your attorney, your attorney may have your friend or family member wait in another room for some or all of the consultation.

3.9 What exactly will my attorney do to help me get a divorce?

Your attorney will play a critical role in helping you get your divorce. You will be actively involved in some of the work, while other actions will be taken behind the scenes at the law office, the law library, or the courthouse.

Your attorney may perform any of the following tasks on your behalf:

- Assess the case to determine which court has jurisdiction to hear the matter
- Develop a strategy for advising you about all aspects of your divorce, including the treatment of assets, spousal support, and matters regarding children
- Counsel you regarding the risks and benefits of negotiated settlement as compared to proceeding to trial
- Help you negotiate an out-of-court settlement when possible
- Prepare legal documents for filing with the court
- Conduct discovery to obtain information from the other party, which could include depositions, requests for production of documents, and written interrogatories
- Appear with you at all court appearances, depositions, and conferences
- Schedule all deadlines and court appearances
- Support you in responding to information requests from your spouse

- Inform you of actions you are required to take
- Perform financial analyses of your case
- Conduct legal research
- Prepare you for court appearances and depositions
- Prepare your case for hearings and trial, including preparing exhibits and interviewing witnesses
- Advise you regarding your rights under the law

As your advocate, your attorney is entrusted to take all of the steps necessary to represent your interests in the divorce.

3.10   What professionals might the court appoint to work with my attorney?

In some cases, in which custody or parenting time issues are seriously disputed, the court may appoint a *guardian ad litem (GAL)*. This is a professional whose duty it is to represent the best interest of the child. A guardian *ad litem* has the responsibility to investigate you and your spouse as well as the needs of your child. The GAL may then be called as a witness at trial to testify regarding any relevant observations.

A similar type of expert is a *parent coordinator (PC)*. A PC is typically appointed only in high-conflict divorces. This person assists in making day-to-day decisions between hearings regarding the children.

Another expert who could be appointed by the court is a *psychologist*. The role of the psychologist will depend upon the purpose for which the psychologist was appointed. For example, the psychologist may be appointed to perform a child-custody evaluation, which involves assessing both parents and the child. Or, this expert may be ordered to evaluate one parent in order to access a child's safety while spending time with that parent.

At times the court will need to hear from financial experts such as asset valuation experts, vocational experts, or tax consultants. These may be court appointed or hired by the parties individually.

3.11 I've been divorced before and I don't think I need an attorney this time; however, my spouse is hiring one. Is it wise to go it alone?

Having gone through a prior divorce, it's likely that you have learned a great deal about the divorce process as well as your legal rights. However, there are many reasons why you should be extremely cautious about proceeding without legal representation.

It is important to remember that every divorce is different. The length of the marriage, whether there are children, the relative financial situation for you and your spouse, as well as your age and health can all affect the financial outcome in your divorce. Further, the person you are divorcing is different. The way that you negotiated with your first spouse may not work with your current spouse.

The law may have changed since your last divorce. Some aspects of divorce law are likely to change each year. New laws get passed and new decisions get handed down by the North Carolina Supreme Court and the North Carolina Court of Appeals that affect the rights and responsibilities of people who divorce. It is also high likely that your judge will be different. Judges have very different judicial philosophies and can vary greatly in their views of families. Attorneys can give insight into how your particular judge handles situations like yours.

In some cases, the involvement of your lawyer could be minimal. This might be the case if your marriage was short, your financial situation very similar to that of your spouse, there are no children, and the two of you remain amicable. At a minimum, have an initial consultation with an attorney to discuss your rights and have an attorney review any final agreement.

3.12 Can I take my children to meetings with my attorney?

It's best to make other arrangements for your children when you meet with your attorney. Your attorney will be giving you a great deal of important information during your conferences, and it will benefit you to give your full attention.

It's also recommended that you take every measure to keep information about the legal aspects of your divorce away from your children. Knowledge that you are seeing an attorney can add to your child's anxiety about the process. It can also make your child a target for questioning by the other parent about your contacts with your attorney.

Most law offices are not designed to accommodate young children and are ordinarily not "childproof." For both your child's well-being and your own peace of mind, explore options for someone to care for your child when you have meetings with your attorney.

3.13 What is the role of the *paralegal* or *legal assistant* in my attorney's office?

A *paralegal,* or *legal assistant,* is a trained legal professional whose duties include providing support for you and your lawyer. Working with a paralegal can make your divorce easier because he or she is likely to be very available to help you. It can also lower your legal costs, as the hourly rate for paralegal services is less than the rate for attorneys.

A paralegal is prohibited from giving legal advice. It is important that you respect the limits of the role of the paralegal if he or she is unable to answer your question because it calls for giving a legal opinion. However, a paralegal can answer many questions and provide a great deal of information to you throughout your divorce.

Paralegals can help you by receiving information from you, reviewing documents with you, providing you with updates on your case, and answering questions about the divorce process that do not call for legal advice.

3.14 My attorney is not returning my phone calls. What can I do?

You have a right to expect your phone calls to be returned by your lawyer. Here are some options to consider:

- Ask to speak to the paralegal or another attorney in the office. Oftentimes your attorney will be out of the office at mediations, depositions, court, or arbitrations. Communicating with the paralegal is often a good (and often less expensive) method to get a message to your attorney.

- Send an e-mail or fax telling your lawyer that you have been trying to reach him or her by phone and explaining the reason it is important that you receive a call.

- Ask the receptionist or paralegal to schedule a phone conference for you to speak with your attorney at a specific date and time.
- Schedule a meeting with your attorney to discuss both the issue needing attention as well as your concerns about the communication.

Your attorney wants to provide good service to you. If your calls are not being returned, take action to get the communication with your lawyer back on track. If the problem persists then you may wish to seek new counsel.

3.15   How do I know when it's time to change lawyers?

Changing lawyers is costly. You will incur legal fees for your new attorney to review information that is already familiar to your current attorney. You will spend time giving much of the same information to your new lawyer as you gave to the one you have discharged. A change in lawyers often results in delays in the divorce.

The following are questions to ask yourself when you're deciding whether to stay with your current attorney or seek new counsel:

- Have I spoken directly to my attorney about my concerns?
- When I expressed concerns, did my lawyer take action accordingly?
- Is my lawyer open and receptive to what I have to say?
- Am I blaming my lawyer for bad behavior of my spouse or opposing counsel?
- Have I provided my lawyer the information needed for taking the next action?
- Does my lawyer have control over the complaints I have, or are they ruled by the law or the judge?
- Is my lawyer keeping promises for completing action on my case?
- Do I trust my lawyer?

- What would be the advantages of changing lawyers when compared to the costs?
- Do I believe my lawyer will support me to achieve the outcome I'm seeking in my divorce?

Every effort should be made to resolve challenges with your attorney. If you have made this effort and the situation remains unchanged, it may be time to switch lawyers.

4

Attorney Fees and Costs

Anytime you make a major investment, you want to know what the cost is going to be and what you are getting for your money. Investing in quality legal representation for your divorce is no different.

The cost of your divorce might be one of your greatest concerns. Because of this, you will want to be an intelligent consumer of legal services. You want quality, but you also want to get the best value for the fees you are paying.

Legal fees for a divorce can be costly and the total expense is not always predictable. But there are many actions you can take to control and estimate the cost. Develop a plan early on for how you will finance your divorce. Speak openly with your lawyer about fees from the outset. Learn as much as you can about how you will be charged. Insist on a written fee agreement.

By being informed, aware, and wise, your financial investment in your divorce will be money well spent to protect your future.

4.1 Can I get free legal advice from a lawyer over the phone?

Every law firm has its own policy regarding lawyers talking to people who are not yet clients of the firm. Most questions about your divorce are too complex for a lawyer to give meaningful answers during a brief phone call.

Questions about your divorce require a complete look at the facts, circumstances, and background of your marriage. To obtain good legal advice, it's best to schedule an initial consultation with a lawyer who handles divorces.

4.2 Will I be charged for an initial consultation with a lawyer?

It depends. While the vast majority of experienced divorce lawyers charge a fee for consultations, there are some attorneys who will offer a free short consultation. If you are getting a free consultation, make sure you know what will be covered. Will the attorney be covering the substantive areas of your case or just letting you get to know the firm? When scheduling your appointment, you should be told the amount of the consultation fee. Sometimes it will be a flat fee or charged at the attorney's hourly rate. Some lawyers charge a "sitting fee" just to meet with them. Payment is ordinarily due at the time of the consultation.

4.3 Will I be expected to give money to the attorney after our first meeting? If so, how much?

If your attorney charges for an initial consultation, be prepared to make payment at the time of your meeting. At the close of your consultation, the attorney may tell you the amount of the retainer needed by the law firm to handle your divorce. However, you are not expected to pay the retainer at the time of your first meeting. Rather, the retainer is paid after you have decided to hire the lawyer, the lawyer has accepted your case, and you are ready to proceed.

4.4 What exactly is a *retainer* and how much will mine be?

A *retainer* is a sum paid to your lawyer in advance for services to be performed and costs to be incurred in your divorce. Some law firms require that you pay a "sitting fee" or true retainer, which is a sum of money that is earned when you hire the attorney. The attorney may also ask for a retainer to be held in their trust account as an advance credit for services that will be charged by the hour as the attorney performs work on your case. For some less contested issues an attorney may offer a "flat fee" such as for the drafting and filing of your uncontested divorce.

If your case is accepted by the law firm, expect the attorney to request a retainer following the initial consultation. The amount of the retainer can be several thousand dollars, depending upon the nature of your case. Contested custody, spousal support cases, divorces involving businesses, or interstate disputes, for example, are all likely to require much higher retainers.

Other factors that can affect the amount of the retainer include the nature and number of the disputed issues, the degree of conflict between the parties, the attorney that your spouse has chosen, and the anticipated overall cost of the litigation.

4.5   I don't have any money and I need a divorce. What are my options?

Two factors to consider in your situation are time and money. Let's look at money first. If your income is very low and your assets are few, you may be eligible to obtain lower costs or free assistance through Child Support Enforcement, local bar-sponsored legal referral services, or other services such as Legal Aid. There are numerous agencies and charities set up to help victims of domestic abuse. Unfortunately, there are not a lot of options to receive free or reduced legal assistance for your divorce in North Carolina.

Child Support Enforcement and Legal Aid have a screening process for potential clients, as well as limits on the nature of the cases they take. The demand for their services is also usually greater than the number of attorneys available to handle cases, and the types of claims they handle are limited. Consequently, if you are eligible for legal services from one of these programs, you should anticipate being on a waiting list. In short, if you have very little income and few assets, you are likely to experience some delay in obtaining a lawyer, if you are even able to get one. If you believe you might be eligible for participation in one of these programs, inquire early to increase your opportunity to get the legal help you are seeking.

4.6   I don't have much money, but I need to get a divorce as quickly as possible. What should I do?

If you have some money and want to get a divorce as soon as possible, consider some of these options:

- Borrow the legal fees from a friend or family member.
- Charge the legal fees on a low-interest credit card.
- Talk with your attorney about using money held in a joint account with your spouse.
- Find an attorney who will work with you on a monthly payment basis.
- Ask your attorney about your spouse paying for your legal fees.
- Contact your county bar organization for a local referral service or a self-help center. Let them know you have some ability to pay and ask for help finding a lawyer who will take your case for a reduced fee.

Even if you do not have the financial resources to proceed with your divorce at this time, consult with an attorney to learn your rights and to develop an action plan for steps you can take between now and the time you are financially able to proceed.

Often there are measures you can take right away to protect yourself until you have the money to proceed with your divorce.

4.7 Is there anything I can do on my own to get support for my children if I don't have money for a lawyer for a divorce?

Yes. If you need support for your children, contact Child Support Enforcement for help in obtaining a child-support order. Although they cannot help you with matters such as custody or property division, they can pursue support from your spouse for your children. Visit their website at www.ncchild-support.com.

4.8 How much does it cost to get a divorce?

The cost of your divorce will depend upon many factors. Some attorneys perform divorces for a flat fee for some simple issues, but most charge by the hour. A flat fee is a fixed amount for the legal services being provided. A flat fee is more likely to be used when there are no children of the marriage and the parties have agreed upon the division of their property and debts. Most North Carolina attorneys charge by the hour for divorces.

It is important that your discussion of the cost of your divorce begin at your first meeting with your attorney. It is customary for family law attorneys to request a retainer, also known as a *fee advance,* prior to beginning work on your case. Be sure to ask your attorney what portion, if any, of the retainer is refundable if you do not continue with the case or terminate your relationship with the attorney.

Attorneys also may take your property division case on a contingency fee. The attorney receives a portion of what you receive from the marital estate. Generally, attorneys combine a contingency fee with an hourly representation; lawyers are not allowed to take contingency fees for issues involving children, an uncontested divorce, or spousal support issues.

4.9   What are typical hourly rates for a divorce lawyer?

In North Carolina, attorneys who practice in the divorce area charge from $200 per hour to more than three times that rate. The rate your attorney charges may depend upon factors such as skills, reputation, experience, and what other attorneys in the area are charging.

If you have a concern about an attorney's hourly rate, but you would like to hire the firm with which the attorney is associated, consider asking to work with an *associate attorney* in the firm who is likely to charge a lower rate. Associates are attorneys who ordinarily have less experience than the senior partners. They are often fully capable of handling your case, as they are usually trained and supervised by the senior partners.

4.10   Can I make payments to my attorney?

Every law firm has its own policies regarding payment arrangements for divorce clients. Often these arrangements are tailored to the specific client. Most attorneys will require a substantial retainer to be paid at the outset of your case. Some attorneys may accept monthly payments in lieu of the retainer. Others may require monthly payments, or request additional retainers as your case progresses. Ask frank questions of your attorney to have clarity about your responsibility for payment of legal fees and make sure your obligations are clearly outlined in a fee agreement.

4.11 I've been turned down by programs providing free legal services. How can I get the money to pay for a lawyer?

There are a number of options to consider when it looks as though you are without funds to pay an attorney. First, look again. Ask yourself whether you have closely examined all sources of funds readily available to you. Are there areas in your budget that can be adjusted to afford an attorney? Sometimes we have simply overlooked money that we might be able to access with ease.

Next, talk to your family members and friends. Often those close to you are concerned about your future and would be very pleased to support you in your goal of having your rights protected. Although this may be uncomfortable to do, remember that most people will appreciate that you trusted them enough to ask for their help. If the retainer is too much money to request from a single individual, consider whether several people might each be able to contribute to help you reach your goal of hiring a lawyer.

If your case is not urgent, consider developing a plan for saving the money you need to proceed with a divorce. Your attorney may be willing to receive and hold monthly payments until you have paid an amount sufficient to pay the initial retainer.

You may also consider taking out a loan or charging your retainer on a credit card. As mentioned, under certain circumstances, an attorney might be willing to be paid from the proceeds of a property settlement through a *contingency fee* or *partial contingency fee*. If you and your spouse have acquired substantial assets during the marriage, you may be able to find an attorney who will wait to be paid until the assets are divided at the conclusion of the divorce.

4.12 I agreed to pay my attorney a substantial retainer to begin my case. Will I still have to make monthly payments?

Ask your attorney what will be expected of you regarding payments on your account while the divorce is in progress. Make sure you understand whether monthly payments on your account will be expected, whether it is likely that you will be asked to pay additional retainers, and whether the firm charges interest on past-due accounts. Most attorneys try to avoid financing their client's cases. Regular payments to your attorney can help you avoid having a tremendously burdensome legal bill at the end of your case.

4.13 My lawyer gave me an estimate of the cost of my divorce and it sounds reasonable. Do I still need a written fee agreement?

Absolutely. Insist upon a written agreement with your attorney. This is essential not only to define the scope of the services for which you have hired your lawyer, but also to ensure that you understand matters such as your attorney's hourly rate, whether you will be billed for certain costs such as copying, and when you can expect to receive statements on your account.

A clear fee agreement reduces the risk of misunderstandings between you and your lawyer. It supports you both in understanding your promises to one another; this way your focus can be on the legal services being provided rather than on disputes about your fees.

4.14 How will I know how the fees and charges are accumulating?

Be sure your written fee agreement with your attorney is completely clear about how you will be informed regarding the status of your account. If your attorney agrees to handle your divorce for a flat fee, your fee agreement should clearly set forth what is included in the fee. If you have questions or are unclear about the fee agreement, be sure to address any confusion with your attorney prior to signing the agreement.

Most attorneys charge by the hour for handling divorces. At the outset of your case, be sure your written fee agreement includes a provision for the attorney to provide you with regular statements of your account. It is reasonable to ask that these be provided monthly.

Review the statement of your account promptly after you receive it. Check to make sure there are no errors, such as duplicate billing entries. If your statement reflects work that you were unaware was performed, call for clarification. Your attorney's office should welcome any questions you have about services it provided. Your statement might also include filing fees, court reporter fees for transcripts of court testimony or depositions, copy expenses, or interest charged on your account.

If several weeks have passed and you have not received a statement on your account, call your attorney's office to request one. Legal fees can mount quickly, and it is important that you stay aware of the status of your legal expenses.

4.15 What other expenses are related to the divorce litigation besides lawyer fees?

Talk to your attorney about costs other than the attorney fees. Ask whether it is likely there will be filing fees, court reporter expenses, subpoenas, or expert-witness fees. Expert-witness fees can be a substantial expense ranging from hundreds to thousands of dollars, depending upon the type of expert and the extent to which the expert is involved in your case.

Speak frankly with your attorney about these costs so that together you can make the best decisions about how to use your budget for the litigation.

4.16 Who pays for the experts such as the appraiser, the accountant, and the psychologist?

Costs for the services of experts, whether appointed by the court or hired by the parties, are ordinarily paid for by the parties. In the case of the guardian *ad litem* who may be appointed to represent the best interest of your children, the amount of the fee will depend upon how much time this professional spends. The judge often orders this fee to be shared by the parties. However, depending upon the circumstances, one party can be ordered to pay the entire fee. If you can demonstrate *indigence,* that is, a very low income and no ability to pay, the county may be ordered to pay your share of the guardian *ad litem* fee.

Psychologists either charge by the hour or they can set a flat fee for a certain type of evaluation. Again, the court can order one party to pay this fee or both parties to share the expense. It is not uncommon for a psychologist to request payment in advance and hold the release of an expert report until fees are paid.

The fees for many experts, including appraisers and accountants, will vary depending upon whether the individuals are called upon to provide only a specific service such as an appraisal, or whether they will need to prepare for giving testimony and appear as a witness at trial.

4.17 What factors will impact how much my divorce will cost?

While it is difficult to predict how much your legal fees will be, the following are some of the factors that affect the cost:

- Is the case is being litigated or is it being settled?
- Is the collaborative law process being used?
- Are there children?
- Is child custody agreed upon?
- Are there novel legal questions?
- Will a pension plan be divided between the parties?
- How many issues have been agreed upon by the parties?
- What is the nature of the contested issues?
- Is there cooperation between the opposing party and opposing counsel?
- Are there litigation costs, such as fees for expert witnesses or court reporters?
- What is the attorney's hourly rate?

Communicating with your lawyer regularly about your legal fees will help you have a better understanding of the overall cost as your case proceeds.

4.18 Will my attorney charge for phone calls and e-mails?

Unless your case is being handled on a flat fee or pure contingency fee basis, you should expect to be billed for phone calls with your attorney. Many of the professional services provided by lawyers are done by phone and by e-mail. This time can be spent giving legal advice, negotiating, or gathering information to protect your interests. These calls and e-mails are all legal services for which you should anticipate being charged by your attorney.

To make the most of your time during attorney phone calls, plan your call in advance. Organize the information you want to relay, your questions, and any concerns to be addressed. This will help you be clear and focused during the phone call so that your fees are well spent.

4.19 Will I be charged for talking to the staff at my lawyer's office?

Typically, yes. Check the terms of your fee agreement with your lawyer. Whether you are charged fees for talking to nonlawyer members of the law office may depend upon their role in the office. For example, many law firms charge for the services of paralegals and law clerks, but not the receptionist.

Remember that nonlawyers cannot give legal advice, so please respect their roles. Do not expect the receptionist to give you an opinion regarding whether you will win custody or receive alimony.

Your lawyer's support staff will be able to relay your messages and receive information from you. They may also be able to answer many of your questions. Allowing support from non-attorneys in the firm also helps control your legal fees.

4.20 What is a *litigation budget,* and how do I know if I need one?

If your case is complex and you are anticipating substantial legal fees, ask your attorney to prepare a *litigation budget* for your review. This can help you to understand the nature of the services anticipated, the time that may be spent, and the overall cost. It can also be helpful for budgeting and planning for additional retainers. Knowing the anticipated costs of litigation can help you to make meaningful decisions about which issues to litigate and which to consider resolving through settlement negotiations.

4.21 What is a *trial retainer* and will I have to pay one?

A *trial retainer* is a sum of money or additional sum to be paid on your account with your lawyer when it appears as though your case may not settle and is at risk for proceeding to trial. The purpose of the trial retainer is to fund the work needed to prepare for trial and for services the day or days of trial.

Confirm with your attorney that any unearned portion of you trial retainer will be refunded if your case settles. Ask your lawyer whether and when a trial retainer might be required in your case so that you can avoid surprise and plan your budget accordingly.

4.22 How do I know whether I should spend the attorney fees my lawyer says it will take to take my case to trial?

Deciding whether to take a case to trial or to settle is often the most challenging point in the divorce process. This decision should be made with the support of your attorney.

When the issues in dispute are primarily financial, often the decision about settlement is related to the costs of going to trial. Make sure you understand just how far apart you and your spouse are on the financial matters and compare this to the estimated costs of going to trial. By comparing these amounts, you can decide whether a compromise on certain financial issues and certainty about the outcome would be better than paying legal fees and not knowing how your case will resolve.

4.23 If my mother pays my legal fees, will my lawyer give her private information about my divorce?

If someone other than you is paying your legal bills, it is important that you be clear with your lawyer and with the person paying that you expect your lawyer to honor the ethical duty to maintain confidentiality. Without your permission, your attorney should not be disclosing information to others about your case unless you consent to it.

If you do want your lawyer to be able to communicate with your family members, advise your lawyer. Expect to be charged by your lawyer for the time spent on these calls or meetings. Regardless of the opinions of the person who pays your attorney fees, your lawyer's duty is to remain your zealous advocate and you are ultimately the decision maker when it comes to your case.

4.24 Can I ask the court to order my spouse to pay my attorney fees?

Yes, for some of the issues of your divorce. In North Carolina you can be awarded some or all of your attorney fees for the issues of contempt, child support, child custody, and spousal support if you are the disadvantaged or dependent party. A *disadvantaged or dependent party* is someone who has less ability to pay legal fees than his or her spouse and someone who is dependent on his or her spouse for support.

If you want to ask the court to order your spouse to pay any portion of your legal fees, be sure to discuss this with your attorney at the first opportunity. Most lawyers will treat the obligation for your legal fees as yours until the other party has made payment.

If your case is likely to require costly experts and your spouse has a much greater ability to pay these expenses than you, talk to your lawyer about the possibility of filing a motion with the court asking your spouse to pay these costs while the case is pending.

4.25 What happens if I don't pay my attorney the fees I promised to pay?

The ethical rules for lawyers allow your attorney to withdraw from representation if you do not comply with your fee agreement. Consequently, it is important that you keep the promises you have made regarding your account and in your fee agreement.

Consider borrowing the funds, using your credit card, or asking for help from friends and family. Most lawyers do not finance their clients' cases. If you are having difficulty paying your attorney fees, talk with your attorney about payment options.

Above all, do not avoid communication with your attorney if you are having challenges making payments. Keeping in touch with your attorney is essential for you to have an advocate at all stages of your divorce.

4.26 Is there any way I can reduce some of the expenses of getting a divorce?

Litigation of any kind can be expensive, and divorces are no exception. The good news is that there are many ways that you can help to control the expense. Here are some of them:

Put it in writing. If you need to relay information that is important but not urgent, consider providing it to your attorney by mail, fax, or e-mail. This creates a prompt and accurate record for your file and your lawyer's file in less time than exchanging phone messages and talking on the phone.

Keep your attorney informed. Just as your attorney should keep you up to date on the status of your case, you need to do the same. Keep your lawyer advised about any major developments in your life (such as plans to move, to have someone move into your home, to change your employment status, or to buy or sell property).

During a divorce, your address, phone number, or e-mail address may change. Be sure to let your attorney know. Often, timely advice on the part of your lawyer can avoid the need for costlier fees later.

Obtain copies of documents. An important part of litigation includes reviewing documents such as tax returns, account statements, report cards, or medical records. Your attorney will ordinarily be able to request or subpoena these items, but many may be more readily available to you.

Consult your attorney's website. If your lawyer has a website, it may be a great source of useful information. The answers to commonly asked questions about the divorce process can often be found there.

Utilize support professionals. Get to know the support staff at your lawyer's office. The receptionist, paralegal, legal secretary, or law clerk may be the person who has the answer to your question. Only the attorneys in the office are able to give you legal advice, but other professionals in the law office can often provide the answers to questions regarding the status of your case. Just as your communication with your attorney, all professionals in a law firm are required to be keep all communications with you strictly confidential.

Consider working with an associate attorney. Although the senior attorneys or partners in a law firm may have more experience, you may find that working with the associate attorney is a good option. Hourly rates for an associate attorney are typically lower than those charged by a senior partner. Frequently, the associate attorney has trained under a senior partner and developed excellent skills as well as knowledge of the law. Many associate attorneys are also very experienced.

Discuss with the firm the benefits of working with a senior or an associate attorney in light of the nature of your case, the expertise of the respective attorneys, and the potential cost savings to you.

Leave a detailed message. If your attorney knows the information you are seeking, he or she can often get the answer before returning your call. This not only gets your answer faster, but also reduces costs.

Discuss more than one matter during a call. It is not unusual for clients to have many questions during litigation. If your question is not urgent, consider waiting to call until you have more than one inquiry. Never hesitate to call to ask any legal questions, especially if they are urgent.

Provide timely responses to information requests. Whenever possible, provide information requested by your lawyer in a timely manner. This avoids the cost of follow-up action by your lawyer and the additional expense of extending the time in litigation.

Carefully review your monthly statements. Scrutinize your monthly billing statements closely. If you believe an error has been made, contact your lawyer's office right away to discuss your concerns.

Remain open to settlement. Be aware that your disagreement about smaller sums of money will often cost more in legal fees to take to court than the value of what is disputed. By doing your part, you can use your legal fees wisely and control the costs of your divorce.

5

The Discovery Process

Interrogatories. Depositions. *Subpoena duces tecum.* Even the words sound foreign. Discovery is one of the least talked about steps in divorce, but it is often among the most important. The discovery process enables you and your spouse to meet on a more level playing field when it comes to settling your case or taking it to trial.

You and your spouse both need the same information if you hope to reach agreement on any of the issues in your divorce. Similarly, the judge must know all of the facts to make a fair decision. The purpose of discovery is to ensure that both you and your spouse have access to the same information. In this way, you can either negotiate a fair agreement or have all of the facts and documents to present to the judge at trial.

The discovery process may seem tedious at times because of the need to obtain and to provide lots of detailed information. Completing it, however, can give tremendous clarity about the issues in your divorce. Trust your lawyer's advice about the importance of having the necessary evidence as you complete the discovery process in order to reach your goals in your divorce.

5.1   What is the actual definition of *discovery?*

Discovery is that part of your divorce process in which the attorneys attempt to learn as much about the facts of your case as possible. Through a variety of methods, both lawyers will request information from you, your spouse, and potential witnesses in your case. Discovery can be informal (probably better described as *voluntary*) or formal. *Informal discovery* is the voluntary exchange of information that can be done either before or after a lawsuit has been filed. *Formal discovery* is done through the court process and under strict *North Carolina Rules of Civil Procedure.*

5.2 What types of *voluntary discovery* might be done by my lawyer or my spouse's lawyer?

Voluntary discovery is just that: voluntary. It consists of requests by one side for disclosure of information by the other side. These requests can be made orally or in writing (letters, e-mails, memorandum) and can seek answers to questions, production of documents, affidavits, photographs, video, audio recordings, or other types of information.

The voluntary exchange of information and documents can save time and money by not having to resort to complex court rules. The problem with voluntary discovery is that, without the court processes to enforce the formal rules, you can never be sure that the information and documentation shared is actually true and complete.

5.3 What types of *formal discovery* might be done by my lawyer or my spouse's lawyer?

Types of *formal discovery* include:

- *Interrogatories*—written questions that must be answered under oath
- *Requests for production of documents*—asking that certain documents be provided by you or your spouse
- *Requests for entry and inspection of property*—which seek the right to go onto and/or look at property
- *Requests for admissions*—asking that certain facts be admitted or denied
- *Subpoena duces tecum*—where the attorney seeks documents from other parties or businesses
- *Depositions*—where questions are asked and answered under oath in the presence of a court reporter but outside of the presence of a judge

Factors that can influence the type of discovery conducted in your divorce can include:

- The types of issues in dispute
- How much access you and your spouse have to needed information
- The level of cooperation in sharing information
- The budget available for performing discovery

Talk to your lawyer about the nature and extent of discovery anticipated in your case.

5.4   How long does the discovery process take?

Discovery can take anywhere from a few weeks to a number of months, depending upon factors such as: the complexity of the case; the cooperation of you and your spouse; and whether expert witnesses are involved.

The *North Carolina Rules of Civil Procedure* provide that interrogatories, *requests for production of documents,* and *requests for admissions* be responded to within thirty days. These rules allow for extensions of time to answer, which are customarily granted (usually for an additional thirty days). Unfortunately, it is not unusual for one side to not answer discovery in a timely manner. In these cases, one side may ask the judge to force the other side to answer the discovery or face serious consequences, called *sanctions.* These sanctions can include payment of the other side's attorney fees, *contempt of court,* or even the judge deciding parts of the case against the sanctioned party without hearing evidence.

5.5   My lawyer insists that we conduct discovery, but I don't want to spend the time and money on it. Is it really necessary?

Yes. The discovery process can be critical to a successful outcome in your case for several reasons:

- It helps to identify the issues in your case.
- It gives information that assists the attorneys in deciding which issues to litigate and which issues to stipulate (agree to).
- It increases the likelihood that any agreements reached are based upon accurate information.
- It provides necessary information for deciding whether to settle or proceed to trial.

- It supports the preparation of defenses by providing information regarding your spouse's case.
- It avoids surprises at trial, such as unexpected witness testimony.

Discuss with your attorney the intention behind the discovery being conducted in your case to ensure it is consistent with your goals and a meaningful investment of your legal fees.

5.6 I just received from my spouse's attorney interrogatories and requests that I produce documents. My lawyer wants me to respond within two weeks. I'll never make the deadline. What can I do?

There are steps you can take to make this task easier. You may even find that you finish before you get to the last steps.

- *Step 1*—Before you do anything else, read all of the questions. Many of them will not apply or your answers will be a simple "yes" or "no."
- *Step 2*—Break it down into smaller tasks. Many of the questions will be easy to answer; get these done quickly. If you answer just a few of the tougher questions a day, the job will not be so overwhelming.
- *Step 3*—Ask a friend or family member to help you. It is important that you develop the practice of letting others help you while you are going through your divorce. Chances are that you will make great progress in just a couple of hours with a friend helping you.
- *Step 4*—Call your lawyer. Ask whether a paralegal in the office can help you organize the needed information or determine whether some of it can be provided at a later date.

Answering your discovery promptly will help move your case forward and help control your legal fees. Delay in the discovery process often leads to frustration by clients and lawyers. Do your best to provide the information in a timely manner with the help of others.

5.7 My spouse has all of my documents. How do I produce them when I do not have them?

The *North Carolina Rules of Civil Procedure* only require production of all requested documents and tangible things that are within a party's possession, custody, or control and that are relevant to the dispute. So the simple answer is: If you do not have a document, you cannot produce it.

But issues in litigation are rarely simple. Your lawyer may, with your assistance and consent, request third parties (those not part of the lawsuit) to produce documents that you have access to (for example, bank statements, phone records, and business records). If the third parties refuse to cooperate, your attorney may use a subpoena to obtain documents that you may not possess, but to which you have access. A *subpoena* is a legal document delivered to a company, person, or witness that requires them to appear in court, appear for a deposition, or produce documents. A third party's failure to comply could result in punishment by the court.

5.8 My spouse's attorneys are asking for documents that seem insignificant to me, and some of the information they are seeking is embarrassing to me. What business is it of theirs?

Almost every person involved in litigation for the first time feels the exact same way. Why is it so complicated? It feels like a violation of privacy. Unfortunately, when someone goes to (or is dragged into) court, much of their privacy is waived by simply arguing their case or defenses. The *North Carolina Rules of Civil Procedure* allows both sides to ask for information "reasonably calculated to lead to the discovery of admissible evidence." Even if the documents or information are not admissible in court, your spouse can ask for it if the information may lead to evidence. This leads to some very broad requests, many of which are acceptable under the law. Make sure to talk to your lawyer about your concerns, because there may be legal objections to the requests that allow you to refuse to produce some information.

5.9   I understand that my spouse's lawyer intends to subpoena my medical records. Aren't these records private?

Whether or not your medical records are relevant in your case will depend upon the issues in dispute. If you are requesting alimony or if your health is an issue in the dispute of child custody, these records may be relevant and discoverable.

Talk with your lawyer about your rights. It may be that a motion to stop the subpoena, known as a *motion to quash* is needed. The nature of the records that can be obtained should be limited to those relevant to your divorce; or that a protective order may be entered to protect you from disclosure of your private medical records to others not involved in the case.

5.10   Can my spouse's attorney force me to produce records from a business that I partially own?

In one way or another, the other side usually can get those records. It may require your spouse's attorney to subpoena the business directly for those records. Typically, the records are produced subject to a protective court order which keeps the records confidential to others not involved in the case.

Many times, it is better (and less expensive) to approach the other owners of the business way before a subpoena is ever issued. Then, you have the chance to explain the situation and take steps to protect the information (such as with a protective order) without the subpoena deadline hanging over your head.

After you have the permission from the other owners, you can produce the documents through discovery yourself rather than involving the business directly in the court process. Using this method can relieve any fears of the other owners without them being served a subpoena by the sheriff without warning.

5.11   It's been two months since my lawyer sent interrogatories to my spouse, and we still don't have his answers. I answered mine on time. Is there anything that can be done to speed up the process?

Yes. Talk with your attorney about filing a *motion to compel,* seeking a court order that your spouse provide the requested information by a certain date. A request for attorney fees for the filing of the motion or other sanctions may be appropriate.

Ask your lawyer whether a subpoena of information from an employer or a financial institution would be a more cost-effective way to get needed facts and documents if your spouse remains uncooperative.

The failure or refusal of a spouse to follow the rules of discovery can add to both the frustration and expense of the divorce process. It is unfair for you to meet every deadline and produce every document when your spouse seems to be an obstructionist.

It may help you to know that judges see this type of bad behavior all of the time and it can affect how they rule on a case. When you act like you have nothing to hide, you are more likely to be believed. When your spouse acts like he or she is hiding information, a judge may scrutinize them more carefully or even distrust them.

5.12 What is a *deposition?*

A *deposition* is the asking and answering of questions under oath, outside of court, in the presence of a court reporter. A deposition may be taken of you, your spouse, or potential witnesses in your divorce case, including experts. Both attorneys will be present. You and your spouse also have the right to be present during the taking of depositions of any witnesses in your case.

Depositions are not performed in every divorce. They are most common in cases involving contested custody, complex financial issues, and expert witnesses.

After your deposition is completed, the questions and answers will be transcribed, that is, typed, by the court reporter exactly as given and bound into one or more volumes.

5.13 What is the purpose of a deposition?

A deposition can serve a number of purposes, such as:

- Supporting the settlement process by providing valuable information
- Helping your attorney determine who to use as witnesses at trial
- Aiding in the assessment of a witness's credibility, that

is, whether the witness appears to be telling the truth

- Helping avoid surprise at trial by learning the testimony of witnesses in advance
- Locking down the testimony of witnesses so they cannot change their testimony at trial
- Preserving testimony in the event a witness becomes unavailable for trial

Depositions can be essential tools in a divorce, especially when a case is likely to proceed to trial.

5.14 Will what I say in my deposition be used against me when we go to court?

Usually, a deposition is used to develop trial strategy and obtain information in preparation for trial. In some circumstances, a deposition may be used at trial.

If you are later called to testify as a witness and give testimony contrary to your deposition, your deposition can be used to impeach you by showing the inconsistency in your statements. It is important to review your deposition prior to your live testimony to ensure consistency and prepare yourself for the type of questions you may be asked.

5.15 Will the judge read the depositions?

Unless a witness becomes unavailable for trial or gives conflicting testimony at trial, it is unlikely that the judge will ever read the depositions.

5.16 How should I prepare for my deposition?

To prepare for your deposition, review the important documents in your case such as the complaint, your answers to interrogatories, and your financial affidavit.

Gather all documents you've been asked to provide at your deposition. Deliver them to your attorney in advance of your deposition for copying and review. Talk to your attorney about the type of questions you can expect to be asked. Discuss with him or her any questions you are concerned about answering.

5.17 What will I be asked? Can I refuse to answer questions?

Questions in a deposition can cover a broad range of topics including your education, work, income, and family. The attorney is allowed to ask anything that is reasonably calculated to lead to the discovery of admissible evidence. If the question may lead to relevant information, it can be asked in a deposition, even though it may be inadmissible at trial. If you are unsure whether to answer a question, ask your lawyer and follow his or her advice.

Your attorney also may object to inappropriate questions. If there is an objection, say nothing until the attorneys discuss the objection. You will be directed whether or not to answer. If there are any questions that you anticipate refusing to answer, you must discuss them with your attorney prior to your deposition. Your attorney can give you some idea about whether you can refuse to answer or not. If you cannot refuse, you and your attorney can plan the best way to approach your answer.

5.18 What if I give incorrect information in my deposition?

You will be under oath during your deposition, so it is very important that you be truthful. If you give incorrect information by mistake, contact your attorney as soon as you realize the error. If you lie during your deposition, you risk being impeached by the other lawyer during your divorce trial. This could cause you to lose credibility with the court, rendering your testimony less valuable.

5.19 What if I don't know or can't remember the answer to a question?

You may be asked questions about which you have no knowledge. It is always acceptable to say "I don't know" if you do not have the knowledge. Similarly, if you cannot remember, simply say so. Many people get themselves in trouble by guessing or speculating the answer to a question, as sometimes the guess is incorrect and later is seen as a lie.

5.20 What else do I need to know about having my deposition taken?

The following suggestions will help you to give a successful deposition:

- Prepare for your deposition by reviewing and providing necessary documents and talking with your lawyer.

- Get a good night's sleep the night before. Eat a meal with protein to sustain your energy, as the length of depositions can vary.

- Arrive early for your deposition so that you have time to get comfortable with your surroundings.

- Relax. You are going to be asked questions about matters you know. Your deposition is likely to begin with routine matters such as your educational and work history.

- Wait for the attorney to ask the question before you start answering. Though normal conversations have interruptions, depositions are not normal conversations. The court reporter will have trouble typing with two people talking at the same time. More importantly, you will not really know what the question is until you have heard the whole question.

- Wait until the question has been asked before you start thinking about your answer.

- Repeat the question silently in your head before answering. This gives your attorney the chance to object to the question, if necessary. It also allows you to make sure you understand the question before you answer it.

- Listen carefully to each question and answer it as asked. Do not try to anticipate what the asking attorney is "really getting at." Each question may be plucked out of the deposition and should, if possible, be able to be understood in its own right. So answer each question concretely, without assumptions.

- If you do not understand the question clearly, ask that it be repeated or rephrased. Do not try to answer what you *think* was asked.

- Answer the question directly. If the question calls only for "yes" or "no," provide such an answer.

- Do not volunteer information. If the lawyer wants to elicit more information, he or she will do so in following questions.
- Tell the truth, including whether you have met with an attorney or discussed preparation for the deposition.
- Stay calm. Your spouse's lawyer will be judging your credibility and demeanor. Do not argue with the attorneys. Take your time and carefully consider the question before answering. There is no need to hurry.
- If you do not know or cannot remember the answer, say so. That is an adequate answer.
- Do not guess.
- If your answer is an estimate or approximation, say so. Do not let an attorney pin you down to anything you are not sure about. For example, if you cannot remember the number of times an event occurred, say that. If the attorney asks you if it was more than ten times, answer only if you can. If you can provide a range (more than ten but less than twenty) with reasonable certainty, you may do so.
- If an attorney mischaracterizes something you said earlier, say so.
- Speak clearly and loudly enough for everyone to hear you.
- Answer all questions with words, rather than gestures or sounds. "Uh-uh" is difficult for the court report to distinguish from "uh-huh" and may result in inaccuracies in the transcript.
- If you need a break at any point in the deposition, you have the right to request one. You can talk to your attorney during such a break.
- Discuss with your lawyer in advance of your deposition whether you should review the transcript of your deposition for its accuracy or whether you should waive your right to review and sign the deposition.

- Remember that the purpose of your deposition is to support a good outcome in your case. Completing it will help your case to move forward.

5.21   Are depositions always necessary? Does every witness have to be deposed?

Depositions are less likely to be needed if you and your spouse are reaching agreement on most of the facts in your case and you are moving toward a settlement. Depositions are more likely to be needed in cases where child custody is disputed or where there are complex financial issues. Although depositions of all witnesses are usually unnecessary, it is common to take the depositions of expert witnesses.

5.22   Will I get a copy of the depositions in my case?

Ask your attorney for copies of the depositions in your case. It will be important for you to carefully review your deposition if your case proceeds to trial.

6

Negotiation and Mediation

If your marriage was full of conflict, you might be asking how you can make the fighting stop. You picture your divorce looking like a scene from the film *War of the Roses,* complete with vicious lawyers and screaming matches. You wonder if there is a way out of this nightmare.

Or, perhaps you and your spouse are parting ways amicably. While you are in disagreement about how your divorce should be settled, you are clear you want the process to be respectful and without hostility. You'd rather spend your hard-earned money on your children's college education than legal fees.

In either case, going to trial and having a judge make all of the decisions in your divorce is not inevitable. In fact, most North Carolina divorce cases settle without the need for a trial.

Negotiation and mediation can help you and your spouse resolve your disputed issues without taking your case before the judge who will make your decisions for you. You reach your own agreements rather than allow the court to make them for you.

Resolving your divorce through a negotiated or mediated settlement has many advantages. You can achieve a mutually satisfying agreement, a known outcome, little risk of appeal, and often enjoy significantly lower legal fees. Despite the circumstances that led to the end of your marriage, it might be possible for your divorce to conclude peacefully with the help of these tools.

Negotiation and Mediation

6.1 What is the difference between *negotiation* and *mediation?*

Both negotiation and mediation are methods used to help you and your spouse settle your divorce by reaching agreement rather than going to trial and having the judge make decisions for you. These methods are two forms of what is sometimes referred to as *alternative dispute resolution* or *ADR.*

Negotiation is when your lawyer and your spouse's lawyer try to resolve some or all of your disputes through a usually informal exchange of information, points of view, settlement offers, and settlement counteroffers. Negotiation has existed as long as people have had disputes, and, at one time, it was the primary way court cases were settled.

A *mediated settlement conference,* or *mediation,* is a type of negotiation that is supervised and facilitated by a trained neutral third party, the "mediator." In the last twenty years, mediation has become a mandatory part of the litigation process. In other words, in most cases, the judge orders the parties to attend a mediation. Before mediation became widely used, a significant portion of cases did not settle until reaching "the courthouse doors," if they settled at all. Some attorneys thought it was a sign of weakness to be the first to contact the opposing party with a reasonable settlement offer. The "fear factor" failed to set in with clients (and attorneys) until the trial was imminent. Mediation was and is a way to get all parties to the negotiating table well before the case goes to trial.

In short, negotiations are settlement talks generally and a mediation is a negotiation conference supervised by a neutral mediator.

6.2 How are negotiation and mediation different from a *collaborative divorce?*

While negotiation and mediation are tools to settle disputes, *collaborative law proceedings* involve an entirely different alternative to litigating in court. In collaborative law proceedings, you and your spouse each hire an attorney trained in the collaborative law process. Both sides and their lawyers enter into an agreement that provides that all parties agree to the collaborative law process. Although the process may be lengthy, it enables the focus to shift away from the conflict and

71

toward finding solutions. The attorneys become a part of the team supporting settlement rather than advocates adding to the conflict.

Talk to your lawyer about whether your case would be well suited to the collaborative law process.

6.3 My lawyer said that negotiation and mediation can reduce delays in completing my divorce. How can they do this?

When the issues in your divorce are decided by a judge instead of by you and your spouse, there are many opportunities for delay. These can include:

- Waiting for a trial date
- Having to return to court on a later, second date if your trial is not completed on the day it is scheduled
- Waiting for the judge's ruling on your case
- Additional court hearings after your trial to resolve disputes about the intention of your judge's rulings, issues that were overlooked, or disagreement regarding language of the judgment

Each one of these events holds the possibility of delaying your divorce by days, weeks, or even months. Mediating or negotiating the terms of your divorce judgments can eliminate these delays.

6.4 How can negotiation and mediation lower the costs of my divorce?

If your case is not settled by agreement, you will be going to trial. If the issues in your case are many or if they are complex, the attorney fees and other costs of going to trial can be tremendous.

By settling your case without going to trial, you may be able to save tens of thousands of dollars in legal fees. Ask your attorney for a litigation estimate that sets forth the potential costs of going to trial, so that you have some idea of these costs when deciding whether to settle an issue or to take it to trial before the judge.

6.5 Are there other benefits to mediating or negotiating a settlement?

Yes. A divorce resolved by a mediated or negotiated agreement can have these additional benefits:

Recognizing common goals. Mediation and negotiation allow for brainstorming between the parties and lawyers. Looking at all possible solutions, even the impractical ones, invites creative solutions to common goals. For example, suppose you and your spouse both agree that you need to pay your spouse some amount of equity for the family home you will keep, but you have no cash to make the payment. Together, you might come up with a number of options for accomplishing your goal and select the best one. Contrast this with the judge who simply orders you to pay the money without considering all of the possible options.

Addressing the unique circumstances of your situation. Rather than using a one-size-fits-all approach as a judge might do, a settlement reached by agreement allows you and your spouse to consider the unique circumstances of your situation in formulating a good outcome. For example, suppose you disagree about the parenting times for the Thanksgiving holiday. The judge might order you to alternate the holiday each year, even though you both would have preferred to have your child share the day with both parents. You and your spouse know your unique situation better than the court and can brainstorm solutions amicably in a settlement.

Creating a safe place for communication. Mediation and negotiation give each party an opportunity to be heard. Perhaps you and your spouse have not yet had an opportunity to share directly your concerns about settlement. For example, you might be worried about how the temporary parenting time arrangement is impacting your children, but have not yet talked to your spouse about it. A mediation session or settlement conference can be a safe place for you and your spouse to communicate your concerns about your children or your finances.

Fulfilling your children's needs. You may see that your children would be better served by you and your spouse deciding their future rather than have it decided by a judge who does not know, love, and understand your children like the two of you do.

Eliminating the risk and uncertainty of trial. If a judge decides the outcome of your divorce, you give up control over the terms of the settlement. The decisions are left in the hands of the judge. If you and your spouse reach agreement, however, you have the power to eliminate the risk of an uncertain outcome.

Reducing the risk of harm to your children. If your case goes to trial, it is likely that you and your spouse will give testimony that will be upsetting to each other. As the conflict increases, the relationship between you and your spouse inevitably deteriorates. This can be harmful to your children. Contrast this with mediation or settlement negotiations, in which you open your communication and seek to reach agreement. It is not unusual for the relationship between the parents to improve as the professionals create a safe environment for rebuilding communication and reaching agreements in the best interest of a child.

Having the support of professionals. Using trained professionals such as mediators and lawyers to support you can help you to reach a settlement that you might think is impossible. These professionals have skills to help you and focus on what is most important to you, and they shift your attention away from irrelevant facts. They understand the law and know the possible outcomes if your case goes to trial.

Lowering stress. The process of preparing for and going to court can be stressful. Your energy should be going toward caring for your children, looking at your finances, and coping with the emotions of divorce. You might decide that you would be better served by settling your case rather than proceeding to trial.

Achieving closure. When you are going through a divorce, the process can feel as though it is taking an eternity. By reaching agreement, you and your spouse are better able to put the divorce behind you and move forward with your lives.

6.6   What types of issues can be negotiated or mediated?

Subject to court-required approval of some types of settlements, all of the issues in your case can be negotiated or mediated. In advance of any mediation or negotiation session, however, you should discuss with your lawyer which issues you want to mediate or negotiate.

You may decide that certain issues are nonnegotiable for you. Discuss your decisions on these issues with your attorney in advance of any negotiation or mediation sessions so that he or she can support you in focusing the discussions on the issues you are open to looking at.

6.7 What is a *settlement conference?*

A *settlement conference* is a meeting held with you, your spouse, and your lawyers with the intention of negotiating the terms of your divorce. In some cases, a professional possessing important information needed to support the settlement process, such as an accountant or other expert, may also participate. A settlement conference held before or after mediation can be a powerful tool for the resolution of your case.

Settlement conferences are most effective when both parties and their attorneys see the potential for a negotiated resolution and have the necessary information to accomplish that goal.

6.8 Why should I consider a settlement conference when the attorneys can negotiate through letters and phone calls?

A settlement conference can eliminate the delays that often occur when negotiation takes place through correspondence and calls between the attorneys. Rather than waiting days or weeks for a response, you can receive a response on a proposal in a matter of minutes.

A settlement conference also enables you and your spouse, if you choose, to use your own words to explain the reasoning behind your requests. You are also able to provide information immediately to expedite the process.

6.9 How do I prepare for my settlement conference?

Being well prepared for the settlement conference can help you make the most of this opportunity to resolve your case without the need to go to trial. Actions you should take include:

- Provide all necessary information in advance of the conference. If your attorney has asked for a current pay stub, tax return, debt amounts, asset values, or other documentation, make sure you have made it available prior to the meeting.

- Discuss your topics of concern with your attorney in advance. Your lawyer can assist you in understanding your rights under the law so that you can have realistic expectations for the outcome of negotiations.

- Bring a positive attitude, a listening ear, and an open mind. Come with the attitude that your case can settle. Be willing to first listen to the opposing party, and then to share your position. To encourage your spouse to listen to your position, listen to hers or his first. Resist the urge to interrupt.

Few cases settle without each side demonstrating flexibility and a willingness to compromise. Most cases settle when the parties are able to bring these qualities to the process.

6.10   What will happen at my settlement conference?

Typically, the conference will be held at the office of one of the attorneys, with both parties and lawyers present. If there are a number of issues to be discussed, an agenda may be used to keep the focus on relevant topics. From time to time throughout the conference, you and your attorney may meet alone to consult as needed. If additional information is needed to reach agreement, some issues may be set aside for later discussion.

The length of the conference depends upon the number of issues to be resolved, the complexity of the issues, and the willingness of the parties and lawyers to communicate effectively. An effort is made to confirm which issues are resolved and which issues remain disputed. Then, one by one, the issues are addressed.

6.11   What is the role of my attorney in the settlement conference?

Your attorney is your advocate during the settlement conference. You can count on him or her to support you throughout the process, to see that important issues are addressed, and to counsel you privately outside of the presence of your spouse and his or her lawyer.

6.12 Why is my lawyer appearing so friendly with my spouse and her lawyer?

Successful negotiations rely upon building trust between the parties working toward agreement. Your lawyer may be respectful or pleasant toward your spouse and your spouse's lawyer to facilitate productive communication and promote a good outcome for you.

6.13 What happens if my spouse and I settled some but not all of the issues in our divorce?

You and your spouse can agree to maintain the agreements you have reached and let the judge decide those matters that you are unable to resolve.

6.14 If negotiation and settlement conferences fail, can I try a mediation to settle the case?

You and your spouse can utilize the mediation process to help resolve any disputes between you. Mediation can occur prior to or after a lawsuit has been filed. If your case is in the court system, it is likely that you will be required to try the mediation process in one form or another.

6.15 What happens at a *mediation?*

A *mediation* is an informal legal proceeding that is facilitated by a *mediator,* a neutral third party. The mediator's sole goal is to help both sides of a dispute reach a mutually agreed-upon settlement. The mediator will not tell you what to do, will not act as a judge, and has no authority to decide your case.

The parties will generally start out together in one room to talk about and identify the issues involved. Many times, the parties (and their attorneys, if they are present) then will separate into private rooms to caucus, brainstorm, and speak freely with the mediator.

The mediator will go from each private room to the other, attempting to relay the perspective of the other side as well as carry offers and counteroffers between the parties. If a settlement is reached, the terms will be written up and signed. If a settlement is not reached on all issues, the case proceeds to trial.

6.16 What is the role of my attorney in the mediation process?

The role of your attorney in the mediation process will vary depending upon your situation and what type of mediation is being utilized. Your attorney can assist you in identifying which issues will be discussed in mediation and which are better left to negotiation or to the judge.

If you have minor children, it is essential that you discuss with your attorney how sharing physical custody of your children can significantly lower child support. In all cases it is important that your attorney review any agreements discussed in mediation before a final agreement is reached.

6.17 Who is the *mediator?*

The *mediator* is a person that has trained in negotiation and mediation techniques. Mediators used in court-ordered mediations must be certified by the State of North Carolina.

The mediator has the power to control the procedure of the mediated settlement conference (who does what next), interpret the rules, and force you to stay until he or she continues the mediation to another day or declares an impasse. The mediator's main duty is to get the case to settle, but he or she cannot force the parties to settle. Rather, the mediator uses persuasion in an attempt to convince each side to settle.

6.18 Is mediation mandatory?

Mediation is not mandatory prior to filing for divorce in North Carolina. Some types of alternative dispute resolution (ADR), including mediation, may be required after filing your lawsuit. Discuss with your attorney what types of ADR will be required in your case and when is a good time to schedule the mediation(s).

6.19 What if a mediation fails?

If a mediation is not successful, you still may be able to settle your case through negotiations between the attorneys, other ADR methods, or even through a subsequent mediation. Also, you and your spouse can agree to preserve the settlements that were reached and to take only the remaining disputed issues to the judge for trial.

6.20 My spouse abused me and I am afraid to participate in a mediation. Should I participate anyway?

If you have been a victim of domestic violence by your spouse, it is important that you discuss the appropriateness of mediation with your attorney. Mediation may not be a safe way for you to reach agreement. If your case has already been filed, talk to your attorney about whether mediation is an appropriate option.

Many mediators will ask you whether you have been a victim of domestic violence prior to allowing mediation to proceed. It is critical for the mediator to both assess your safety and to ensure that the balance of power in the mediation process is maintained.

If you feel threatened or intimidated by your spouse, but still want to proceed with mediation, talk to your attorney about filing court papers that would allow him or her to attend the mediation sessions with you. Request to have the mediation occur at your lawyer's office, where you feel more comfortable. Also ask about mediating with your spouse being in a separate room. If you do participate in mediation, insist that your mediator have a good understanding of the dynamics of domestic abuse and how they can impact the mediation process.

If you do not wish to attend a mediation, ask your lawyer about other alternative dispute resolution options that may help resolve your case without having to have a trial.

6.21 What are the different kinds of alternative dispute resolution (ADR) used in family courts?

North Carolina requires custody mediation and a choice of one other ADR to be used in the divorce litigation process. The types of ADR that you may choose consist of *family financial settlement program mediation, judicial settlement conference,* and *early neutral evaluation.*

6.22 What is the *custody mediation program?*

The *custody mediation program* addresses issues of child custody and visitation. After a case involving custody or visitation is filed, the case is sent to the custody mediation program.

The court then orders the parties to attend an orientation session and at least one custody mediation.

6.23   How do I prepare for a custody mediation?

Prior to attending a custody mediation session with your spouse, discuss with your attorney the issues you intend to mediate. In particular, be sure to discuss the impact of custody and parenting time arrangements on child support.

Enlist your attorney's support in identifying your intentions for the mediation. Make a list of the issues important to you. For example, when it comes to your child, you might consider whether it is your child's safety, the parenting time schedule, or the ability to attend your children's events that concerns you most.

Be forward looking. Giving thought to your desired outcomes while approaching mediation with an open mind and heart is the best way to move closer to settlement.

6.24   What is involved in the custody mediation process? What will I have to do and how long will it take?

Though the details vary from county to county, usually within thirty days of the case arriving at the custody mediation program, an orientation is scheduled. In a group class, the orientation prepares you for the custody mediation.

In the custody mediation, the mediator will meet with you and your spouse alone, without anyone else present, including your lawyers. A custody mediation lasts around two hours. If all parties (including the mediator) agree, additional sessions can be scheduled.

Custody mediation sessions are private. Only the parties named in the lawsuit are present for mediation. Unless the mediator witnesses a crime, hears a criminal threat, or is concerned about child abuse, the mediator will not tell anyone (including the judges and attorneys) about what is discussed in the custody mediation process.

If everyone agrees to a plan, a parenting agreement is drafted by the mediator. If everything is not agreed upon in the custody mediation, the case proceeds to the court for trial.

6.25 I want my attorney to look over the agreements my spouse and I discussed in the custody mediation before I give my final approval. Is this possible?

Yes. Before giving your written or final approval to any agreements reached in a custody mediation, it is critical that your attorney review the agreements first. This is necessary to ensure that you understand the terms of the settlement and its implications. Your attorney will also review the agreement for compliance with North Carolina law.

6.26 If we settle at a custody mediation, what happens next?

After the parties and their attorneys have reviewed the parenting agreement, the parenting agreement is signed and presented to the judge for his or her signature, incorporating it into a court order.

6.27 Who chooses the mediator and pays for the custody mediation?

Currently, the state of North Carolina assigns and pays the mediator for the custody mediation.

6.28 Will the courts allow a custody mediation to be waived?

Custody mediations may be waived by court order if either side proves undue hardship. Some examples of undue hardship are: living more than fifty miles away from the court; abuse or neglect of the minor children; abuse of a spouse by the other spouse; severe psychological, psychiatric, or emotional problems; and alcoholism or drug abuse by one of the parties. Custody mediations may also be waived if both sides agree to a private mediation.

6.29 What is a *family financial settlement mediation?*

The *family financial settlement program mediations* help parties deal with the financial side of divorce, including division of marital property, claims for alimony, and child support. It is common for child-custody and visitation issues to also be handled at family financial settlement mediations.

6.30 Regarding *family financial settlement program mediations,* what is involved in the mediation process? What will I have to do and how long will it take?

The mediation process will be explained to you in detail by your lawyer well before the mediation. The mediator also will explain the process at the start of the *mediated settlement conference.*

The mediator will outline ground rules designed to ensure you will be treated respectfully and given an opportunity to be heard. In most cases your attorney and your spouse's attorney will each be given an opportunity to make some opening remarks about the case from each side's perspective. After the opening remarks, each side will continue to communicate how they view the case until the mediator decides face-to-face communication is no longer productive. At this time, the mediator will have each side go to separate rooms for "break-out sessions."

During the break-out sessions, the mediator will meet separately with each side to describe the latest settlement offer from your spouse, to listen to you and your attorney's thoughts about the offer, and to encourage your to make a new settlement counteroffer. Then the mediator takes your counteroffer to the room with your spouse, repeating the same process. This continues until the case is settled, the mediator decides to "hold the mediation open" (which means the mediation will continue at a later date), or the mediator declares an impasse (stops the mediation and tells the court that the case did not settle at mediation).

The length of time the process of mediation continues depends upon many of the same factors that affect how long your divorce will take. These include how many issues you and your spouse disagree about, the complexity of these issues, and the willingness of each of you to work toward an agreement. These type of mediations commonly last all day, though some end more quickly.

6.31 Can we decide nonfinancial matters at the family financial settlement program mediation?

Yes. You and your spouse can discuss and (hopefully) settle any disputes you may have during the mediation.

6.32 Who picks the mediator for a family financial settlement program mediation?

If they can agree on one, the parties and their attorneys select the mediator. If they cannot agree on a mediator, the court will appoint a mediator from a list of mediators certified by the state of North Carolina.

6.33 Who pays for the family financial settlement program mediation?

If the parties select their own mediator, the mediator's fees are determined by agreement between the parties and the mediator. If the court must appoint the mediator, then the parties will split the $150 administrative fee as well as the $150 per hour paid to the mediator.

6.34 What is a *judicial settlement conference?*

A *judicial settlement conference* is a proceeding attended by all the parties and their attorneys and that is led by a district court judge who is not the judge assigned to the case. Generally, the judge conducting the conference decides the details of how the case proceeds. The judge does not force the parties to settle the case. Rather, the judge will try to persuade the parties to resolve all of their differences. The settlement conference is confidential and the judge is not allowed to talk to the trial judge about what occurred at the settlement conference.

6.35 What is an *early neutral evaluation?*

Early neutral evaluations involve an informal conference in which each side presents abbreviated written and oral summaries of the case to a neutral evaluator. The evaluator offers a nonbinding, oral opinion of each party's case and a candid assessment of the possible outcome of the case if it proceeds to trial. Early neutral evaluations are rarely utilized in North Carolina.

7

Emergency:
When You Fear Your Spouse

Suddenly you are in a panic. Maybe your spouse was serious when he said he would take your child and leave the state. Is your spouse threatening to hurt you? What if you are kicked out of your own home? Suppose all of the bank accounts are emptied. Your fear heightens as your mind spins with all of the possibilities from every horror story you ever heard about divorce.

Facing an emergency situation in divorce can feel as though your entire life is at stake. You may not be able to concentrate on anything else. At the same time, you may be paralyzed with anxiety and have no idea how to begin to protect yourself. No doubt you have countless worries about what your future holds.

Remember that you have overcome many challenges in your life before this moment. There are people willing to help you. You have strength and wisdom you may not yet even realize. Step by step, you will make it through this time.

When facing an emergency, do your best to focus on what to do in the immediate moment. Set aside your worries about the future for another day. Now it is time to stay in the present moment, let others support you, and start taking action right away.

7.1 My spouse has deserted me, and I need to get divorced as quickly as possible. What is my first step?

Your first step is to get legal advice as soon as possible. The earlier you get legal counsel to advise you about your rights, the better. The initial consultation will answer most of your questions and start you on an action plan for getting your divorce underway.

7.2 I'm afraid my abusive spouse will try to hurt me and/or our children if I say I want a divorce. What can I do legally to protect myself and my children?

Develop a plan with your safety and that of your children as your highest priority. In addition to meeting with an attorney at your first opportunity, develop a safety plan in the event you and your children need to escape your home. A great way to do this is to let in support from an agency that helps victims of domestic violence. Call the Women Against Violence Hotline at (800) 799-SAFE (7233) or visit the website at www.thehotline.org to get more information about the domestic violence program closest to you. Your risk of harm from an abusive spouse increases when you leave. For this reason, all actions must be taken with safety as the first concern.

Find a lawyer who understands domestic violence. Often your local domestic violence agency can help with a referral. Talk to your lawyer about the concerns for your safety and that of your children. Ask your lawyer about a *domestic violence restraining order.* This is a court order that may offer a number of protections including granting you temporary custody of your children for up to one year and ordering your spouse to leave the family residence and have no contact with you.

7.3 I am afraid to meet with a lawyer because I am terrified my spouse will find out and get violent. What should I do?

Schedule an initial consultation with an attorney who is experienced in working with domestic violence victims. When you schedule the appointment, let the firm know your situation and instruct the law office not to place any calls to you that you think your spouse might discover.

Consultations with your attorney are confidential. Your lawyer has an ethical duty not to disclose your meeting with anyone outside of the law firm. Let your attorney know your concerns so that extra precautions can be taken by the law office in handling your file. You may want to consider having a friend or family member pay for your consultation or give you cash to pay for your consult.

7.4 I want to give my attorney all the information needed so my children and I are safe from my spouse. What does this include?

Provide your attorney with complete information about the history, background, nature, and evidence of your abuse including:

- The types of abuse (for example, physical, sexual, verbal, financial, mental, emotional)
- The dates, time frames, locations, or occasions of abuse
- The specific incidents of abuse
- Whether you were ever treated medically
- Any police reports made
- E-mails, letters, notes, or journal entries
- Any photographs taken
- Any witnesses to the abuse or evidence of the abuse
- Any statements made by your spouse admitting the abuse
- Any damaged property
- Injuries you or your children suffered
- Any counseling you had because of the abuse
- Alcohol or drug abuse
- The presence of guns or other weapons

The better the information you provide to your lawyer, the easier it will be for him or her to make a strong case for the protection of you and your children. It is important to treat threats as well as physical abuse seriously and with urgency. Contact your attorney as soon as it is safe to do so. If you are in immediate danger call the police or go to your magistrate to get immediate assistance.

7.5   I'm not ready to hire a lawyer for a divorce, but I am afraid my spouse is going to get violent with my children and me in the meantime. What can I do?

It is possible to seek a protective order from the court without an attorney. It is possible for the judge to order your spouse out of your home, granting you custody of your children, and order your spouse to stay away from you. Typically, this first hearing is done *ex parte*, that is, without your spouse there. There will be a return hearing that occurs within ten days of your *ex parte* hearing. It is best to have an attorney with you at the return hearing to ensure that your temporary order is extended for up to one year.

7.6   What's the difference between a *protective order* and a *restraining order*?

Restraining orders are court orders directing a person not to engage in certain behavior, such as harassing and threatening a spouse. A *protective order* is usually referred to as a *domestic violence protective order (DVPO)*, a specific type of restraining order that is intended to protect victims of domestic violence. In addition to targeting domestic violence through a DVPO, restraining orders can be issued to prevent a non-abusive spouse from draining marital bank accounts, from speaking negatively about the spouse in front of the children, and from a number of other acts that would be damaging to the other spouse or the children.

Although either a DVPO or a restraining order can initially be obtained without notice to the other spouse, that spouse always has a right to a hearing to determine whether a protective order or restraining order should remain in place.

Talk to your attorney about obtaining a DVPO if you are concerned about your safety and the safety of your children or if there has been a history of domestic violence. The violation of a protective order is a criminal offense which can result in immediate arrest.

If you are concerned that your spouse will do things that will cause irreparable harm to you, your family, or the marital estate after your divorce complaint is filed, ask your lawyer about a restraining order. If your spouse violates the restraining order, he or she may be brought before the court for contempt.

7.7 My spouse has never been violent, but I know she is going to be really angry and upset when the divorce papers are served. Do I need a protective order?

The facts of your case may not warrant a protective order. Generally, you or a household member must be a victim of past domestic violence or "in fear of imminent serious bodily injury or continued harassment that rises to such a level as to inflict substantial emotional distress" to obtain a domestic violence protective order. If, however, you are concerned about your spouse's behavior (even if you do not believe you qualify for a DVPO), ask your attorney about what steps you can take to protect yourself.

7.8 My spouse says I am crazy, that I am a liar, and that no judge will ever believe me if I tell the truth about the abusive behavior. What can I do if I don't have any proof?

Most domestic violence is not witnessed by third parties. Often there is little physical evidence. Even without physical evidence, a judge can enter orders to protect you and your children if you give truthful testimony about your abuse which the judge finds believable. Your own testimony of your abuse is evidence.

It is very common for persons who abuse others to claim that their victims are liars and to make statements intended to discourage disclosure of the abuse. This is yet another form of controlling behavior.

Your attorney's skills and experience will support you to give effective testimony in the courtroom to establish your case. Let your lawyer know your concerns so that a strong case can be presented to the judge based upon your persuasive statements of the truth of your experience.

7.9 I'm afraid my spouse is going to take all of the money out of the bank accounts and leave me with nothing. What can I do?

Talk to your attorney immediately. If you are worried about your spouse emptying financial accounts or selling marital assets, it is critical that you take action at once. Your attorney can advise you on your right to take possession of certain assets in order to protect them from being hidden or spent by your spouse.

Ask your lawyer about seeking a *temporary restraining order (TRO)* to protect your assets. This order forbids your spouse to sell, transfer, hide, or otherwise dispose of marital property until the divorce is complete. A temporary restraining order is intended to prevent assets from "disappearing" before a final division of the property from your marriage is complete. You also may ask for an interim distribution of your marital property. The court can divide up accounts prior to a final hearing. Often you can get into court within thirty to sixty days for these types of hearings.

7.10 My spouse told me that if I ever file for divorce, I'll never see my child again. Should I be worried about my child being abducted?

Your fear that your spouse will abduct your child is a common one. It can be helpful to look at some of the factors that appear to increase the risk that your child will be removed from the state by the other parent.

Most child abductions are committed by men. Child abductions occur more often in marriages in which the parents come from different cultures, races, religions, or ethnic backgrounds. Other factors that increase risk of abduction are lower socioeconomic status, prior criminal record, and limited social or economic ties to the community.

Mental manipulation, bordering on brainwashing of a child, is almost always present in cases involving a child who is at risk for being kidnapped by a parent. The offending parent also usually makes efforts to isolate the child from other relatives. Other indicators may include obtaining a passport, getting financial matters in order, or contacting a moving company.

Talk to your lawyer to assess the risks in your case. Together you can determine whether statements and threats by your spouse are intended to control or intimidate you or whether you need to take legal action to protect your child. If there is strong evidence that a child is being physically abused or your spouse is trying to evade the jurisdiction of the court, you may be entitled to seek an emergency custody order.

7.11 What legal steps can be taken to prevent my spouse from removing our child from the state?

If you are concerned about your child being removed from the state, talk to your lawyer about whether any of these options might be available in your case:

- A court order giving you immediate custody until a temporary custody hearing can be held
- A court order directing your spouse to turn over passports for the child and your spouse to the court
- The posting of a bond prior to your spouse exercising parenting time
- Supervised visitation

Both state and federal laws are designed to provide protection from the removal of children from one state to another when a custody matter is brought and to protect children from kidnapping. The *Uniform Child Custody Jurisdiction Enforcement Act (UCCJEA)* was passed to encourage the custody of children to be decided in the state where they have been living most recently and where they have the most ties. The *Parental Kidnapping Prevention Act (PKPA)* makes it a federal crime for a parent to kidnap a child in violation of a valid custody order.

If you are concerned about your child being abducted, talk with your lawyer about all options available to you for your child's protection.

7.12 If either my spouse or I file for divorce, will I be ordered out of my home? Who decides who gets to live in the house while we go through the divorce?

This is one of the most common and most difficult questions among people going through a divorce. In North Carolina there are no quick and easy ways to resolve this kind of dispute. Absent spousal or child abuse, removing a spouse from a residence could take months or years if at all.

If you and your spouse cannot reach an agreement regarding which of you will leave the residence during the divorce, then under certain circumstances the judge will decide whether one of you should be granted exclusive possession of the home until the case is concluded. In many cases judges have been known to refuse to order either party out of the house until the divorce is concluded.

Abusive behavior is one basis for seeking immediate temporary possession of the home. If there are minor children, the custodial parent may be awarded temporary possession of the residence. Other factors the judge may consider include:

- Either party's commitment of fault during the marriage, such as alcohol/ drug abuse, adultery, and/ or causing the other spouse's life to be burdensome and intolerable
- Whether one of you owned the home prior to the marriage
- After provisions are made for payment of temporary support, who can afford to remain in the home or obtain other housing
- Who is most likely to be awarded the home in the divorce
- Options available to each of you for other temporary housing, including other homes or family members who live in the area
- Special needs that would make a move unduly burdensome, such as a health condition

If staying in the home is important to you, talk to your attorney about your reasons so that a strong case can be made for you.

8

Child Custody

Ever since you and your spouse began talking about divorce, chances are your children have been your greatest concern. You or your spouse might have postponed the decision to seek divorce because of concern about the impact on your children. Now that the time has come, you might still have doubts about how the divorce will affect your children in the long term.

Remember that you have been making wise and loving decisions for your children since they were born. You have always done your best to see that they had everything they really needed. You loved them and protected them. This will not change simply because you are going through your divorce. You were a good parent before the divorce and you will be a good parent after the divorce.

It can be difficult not to worry about how the sharing of parenting time with your spouse will affect your children. You may also have fears about being cut out of your child's life. Try to remember that regardless of who has custody, it is likely that the court order will not only give you a lot of time with your children but also a generous opportunity to be involved in their day-to-day lives.

With the help of your lawyer, you can make sound decisions regarding the custody arrangement that is in the best interest of your children. This chapter focuses primarily on what happens in the court process. Most parents, experts, and lawyers agree that resolving the issues related to your children out of court is far better for your children, you, and your spouse. A settlement of custody issues that each party agrees to is likely to provide for a more stable and long-lasting resolution for your family, rather than one imposed upon you by a judge.

8.1 What types of custody are awarded in North Carolina?

Under North Carolina law, there are two aspects to a custody determination: "legal custody" and "physical custody." *Legal custody* refers to the power to make important long-lasting decisions regarding your children. Legal custody may be awarded to you, to your spouse, or to both of you jointly.

If you have *sole legal custody,* you are the primary and final decision maker for significant long lasting matters regarding your children, such as which school they attend, religious issues, and who their health care providers are. The noncustodial parent will have parenting time and other rights.

Joint legal custody means that you and your former spouse will share equally in the decision making for your child. If you and the other parent are unable to reach agreement, you may need to return to mediation or to court for the decision to be made.

Joint legal custody may not be appropriate unless certain factors are present, such as:

- Effective and open communication between the parents concerning the child
- A strong desire on the part of both parents to continue to co-parent together
- A history of active involvement of both parents in the child's life
- Similar parenting values held by both parents
- A willingness on the part of both parents to place the child's needs before their own
- Both parents' willingness to be flexible and compromising about making decisions concerning the child

Physical custody refers to the physical location of the children—where they spend their time. Like legal custody, it may be awarded to either parent or to both parents jointly.

Joint physical custody is sometimes referred to as *shared physical custody.*

Specific parenting time should always be awarded to each parent, regardless of who has physical custody. Provisions for days of the week, school breaks, summer, holidays, and vacations are typically made in detail. In the event that one of your children will reside with you and another child will reside with the other parent, the arrangement is referred to as *split physical custody.*

If you are considering joint physical custody, be sure to discuss with your attorney not only the best interest of your child, but also the possible ramifications of joint physical custody to child support. An award of joint (shared) physical custody can result in a reduction in direct child support.

8.2   On what basis will the judge award custody?

The judge considers many factors in determining child custody. Most important is "the best interest of the child." This approach is child-centric and not parent-centric. It is key to understand that the judge will want to preserve the child's relationship with both parents, while reducing unnecessary disruptions to the child's routine. To determine best interest, the judge may look at the factors described below.

Home environments. This refers to the respective environments offered by you and your spouse. The court may consider factors such as the safety, stability, and nurturing found in each home.

Emotional ties. The emotional relationship between your child and each parent may include the nature of the bond between the parent and child and the feelings shared between the child and each parent.

Age, sex, and health of the child and parents. North Carolina no longer ascribes to the "tender years" doctrine, which formerly gave a preference for custody of very young children to the mother. The judge, therefore, will consider both the father and the mother for custody. If one of the parents has an illness that may impair the ability to parent, it may be considered by the court. Similarly, the judge may look at special health needs of a child.

Effect on the child of continuing or disrupting an existing relationship. This factor might be applied in your case if you stayed at home for a period of years to care for your child, and awarding custody to the other parent would disrupt your relationship with your child.

Promotion of the minor child's relationship with the other parent. The court may consider your ability and willingness to be cooperative with the other parent in deciding who should be awarded custody. The court will pay close attention to how the parties communicate and promote the other parent's relationship with the minor children. Treating the other spouse negatively in front of the minor children can greatly affect your ability to achieve your custody goals.

Capacity to provide physical care and satisfy educational needs. Here the court may examine whether you or the other parent is better able to provide for your child's daily needs such as nutrition, health care, hygiene, social activities, and education.

Comfort and routines of the minor child. What has been occurring during the marriage is very important to determine what kind of parenting schedule the court will award. The judge may consider who had been providing the children's needs in the past and the particular routines and needs of the minor children. The court may also look to see how and whether you or your spouse have been attending to these needs in the past.

While what the parents did throughout the marriage to provide for the comfort and routine of the child is an important factor, it is often as important to show the routine since the separation. Each parent has equal rights to parenting the child, making it difficult to set up a schedule or routine that works for both parents. If a routine since separation has been working for the minor child, the judge may weigh that information strongly.

Preferences of the child. The child's preference regarding custody will be considered if the child is of sufficient age of comprehension, regardless of chronological age, and the child's preference is based on sound reasoning. North Carolina, unlike some other states, does not allow a child to unilaterally choose the parent he or she wishes to live with. Rather, at any age the court may consider the well-reasoned preferences of a child. Typically, the older the child, the greater the weight given to the preference. The child's reasoning is also important. Ultimately, the judge makes the decision based on all of the evidence. Having a child testify is extremely stressful for the child and should be avoided if possible.

Health, welfare, and social behavior of the child. Every child is unique. Your child's needs must be considered when it comes to deciding custody and parenting time. The custody of a child with special needs, for example, may be awarded to the parent who is better able to meet those needs.

The judge may also consider whether you or your spouse has fulfilled the role of primary care provider for meeting the day-to-day needs of your child.

The ability to show a plan to provide for the physical and emotional well-being of the minor child going forward is essential. Proper supervision by a parent or someone designated by the parent, such as an after-school child-care provider, is essential. It is best to be able to articulate how you can provide for the day-to-day needs going forward.

Domestic violence. Domestic violence is an important factor in determining custody, as well as parenting time and protection from abuse during the transfer of your child to the other parent. If domestic violence is a concern in your case, be sure to discuss it in detail with your attorney during the initial consultation so that every measure can be taken to protect the safety of you and your children.

8.3 What's the difference between *visitation* and *parenting time?*

Historically, time spent with the noncustodial parent has been referred to as *visitation.* Today, the term *parenting time* is used to refer to the time a child spends with either parent. This change in language reflects the intention that children spend time with both parents and have two homes, as opposed to their living with one parent and visiting the other.

8.4 How can I make sure I will get to keep the children during the divorce proceedings?

Until an order of custody is entered in North Carolina, each parent has equal rights to custody and parenting time for their children. A temporary court order is the best way to be sure your children will stay with you while your divorce is proceeding. Even if you and your spouse have agreed to temporary arrangements, talk with your attorney about whether this agreement should be formalized in a court order so that it can be enforced.

Obtaining a temporary order can be an important protection not only for the custody of your children, but for other issues such as support and temporary exclusive possession of the marital home.

Until a temporary order is entered, it's best that you continue to reside with your children if obtaining custody of them is important to you. It is usually recommended that the children stay in the family home. If you must leave your home, first talk with your attorney about your options such as taking your children with you and seeking the appropriate court orders. These might include orders for temporary protection, custody, support, possession of your home, or attorney fees.

Prior to disrupting your children's routine, you need to develop a strategy on how to get an appropriate temporary order and whether you will be able to retake possession of the marital home.

8.5   How much weight does the child's preference carry?

The preference of your child is only one of many factors a judge considers in determining custody. Although there is no age at which your child's preference determines custody, most judges give more weight to the wishes of an older child.

The reasoning underlying your child's preference is also a factor to consider. Consider the fifteen-year-old girl who wants to live with her mother because "Mom lets me stay out past curfew, I get a bigger allowance, and I don't have to do chores." Greater weight might be given to the preference of an eight-year-old who wants to live with his mother because "she helps me with my homework, reads me bedtime stories, and doesn't call me names like Dad does."

If you see that your child's preference may be a factor in the determination of custody, discuss it with your lawyer so that this consideration is a part of assessing the action to be taken in your case. You should consider the emotional and psychological effects of having your child testify. Some judges view a parent negatively for requiring a child to testify about their preferences.

8.6   How can I prove that I was the primary care provider?

One tool to assist you and your attorney in establishing your case as a primary care provider is a Parental Roles Chart indicating the care you and your spouse have each provided for your child. The clearer you are about the history of parenting, the better job your attorney can do in presenting your case to the judge. Look at the activities in the chart to help you review the role of you and your spouse as care providers for your child.

Parental Roles Chart

Activity	Mother	Father
Attended prenatal medical visits		
Attended prenatal class		
Took time off work after child was born		
Got up with child for feedings		
Got up with child when sick at night		
Bathed child		
Put child to sleep		
Potty-trained child		
Prepared and fed meals to child		
Helped child learn numbers, letters, colors		
Helped child learn to read		
Helped child with practice for sports, dance, music		
Took time off work for child's appointments		
Stayed home from work with sick child		
Took child to doctor visits		
Went to pharmacy for child's medication		
Administered child's medication		
Took child to therapy		
Took child to optometrist		

Parental Roles Chart (Continued)

Activity	Mother	Father
Took child to dentist		
Took child to get haircuts		
Bought clothing for child		
Bought school supplies for child		
Transported child to school		
Picked child up after school		
Drove carpool for child's school		
Went to child's school activities		
Helped child with homework and projects		
Attended parent–teacher conferences		
Helped in child's classroom		
Chaperoned child's school trips and activities		
Transported child to day care		
Attended day care activities		
Transported child from day care		
Signed child up for sports, dance, music		
Bought equipment for sports, dance, music		
Attended sports, dance, music recitals		
Coached child's sports		
Transported child from sports, dance, music		
Knows child's friends and friends' families		
Took child to religious education		
Obtained information and training about special needs of child		
Comforted child during times of emotional upset		

8.7 Do I have to let my spouse see the children before we are actually divorced?

In North Carolina each parent has equal rights to custody of the children until an order is entered setting up the parent's respective rights to custody and parenting time. Unless your children are at risk of being harmed by your spouse, your children should maintain regular contact with the other parent. If your children are at risk for harm from your spouse you should seek legal help immediately to get a temporary or emergency order to protect them and yourself.

It is important for children to experience the presence of both parents in their lives, regardless of the separation of the parents. Even if there is no temporary order for parenting time, cooperate with your spouse in making reasonable arrangements for time with your children.

When safety is not an issue, if you deny contact with the other parent prior to trial, your judge is likely to question whether you have the best interest of your child at heart. North Carolina law makes it clear that a factor in determining whether a parent should be the primary caregiver going forward is whether that parent has promoted the child's relationship with the other parent. Talk to your spouse or your lawyer about what parenting time schedule would be best for your children on a temporary basis.

8.8 I am seeing a psychotherapist. Will that hurt my chances of getting custody?

If you are seeing a therapist, commend yourself for getting the professional support you need. Your well-being is important to your ability to be the best parent you can be.

Talk with your lawyer about the implications of your being treated by a therapist. It may be that the condition for which you are being treated in no way affects your child or your ability to be a loving and supportive parent.

Your mental health records may be subpoenaed by the other parent's lawyer. For this reason, it is important to discuss with your attorney an action plan for responding to a request to obtain records in your therapist's file. Ask your attorney to contact your therapist to alert him or her regarding how to respond to a request for your mental health records.

8.9 Can having a live-in partner hurt my chances of getting custody?

Your living with someone who is not your spouse may have serious impact on your custody case, but judges' opinions of the significance of this factor can vary greatly. If you are contemplating having your partner live with you, discuss your decision with your attorney first. If you are already living with your partner, let your attorney know right away so that the potential impact on any custody ruling can be assessed.

Talk promptly and frankly with your lawyer. It will be important that the two of you look together at many aspects, including the following:

- How the judge assigned to your case views this situation
- Whether your living arrangement is likely to prompt a custody dispute that would otherwise not arise
- How long you have been separated from the other parent
- How long you have been in a relationship with your new partner
- The history and nature of the children's relationship with your partner
- Whether your partner poses any significant risk to your children or has historical risk factors such as: a criminal record, substance abuse issues, prior domestic or violence issues
- Your future plans with your partner (such as marriage)

Living with a partner may put your custody case at risk. Consider such a decision thoughtfully, after taking into account the advice of your lawyer.

8.10 Will all the sordid details of my or my spouse's affair have to come out in court in front of our children?

Judges make every effort to protect children from the conflicts between their parents. For this reason, most judges typically will not allow children to be present in the courtroom to hear the testimony of other witnesses. Although the risk that your spouse may share information with your child cannot be eliminated, it would be highly unusual for a judge to allow a child to hear such testimony in a courtroom.

8.11 Should I hire a private detective to prove my spouse is having an affair?

It depends. If custody is disputed and your spouse is having an affair, discuss with your attorney how a private investigator might help you gather evidence to support your case. Discuss the following considerations with your attorney:

- What view on extramarital relationships does my judge hold?
- How is the affair affecting the children?
- How much will a private investigator cost?
- Will the evidence gathered help my case?
- Are there other issues or claims that will be helped by "proving" that your spouse committed adultery?

Your attorney can help you determine whether hiring a private investigator is a good idea in your particular case.

8.12 Will the fact that I had an affair during the marriage hurt my chances of getting custody?

Whether a past affair will have any impact on your custody case will depend upon many factors, including:

- The views of the judge assigned to your case
- Whether the affair had any impact on the children
- How long ago the affair occurred
- The quality of the evidence about the affair
- The character of the person you had an affair with

If you had an affair during your marriage, discuss it with your attorney at the outset so that you can discuss its impact, if any, on custody.

8.13 During the months it takes to get a divorce, is it okay to date or will it hurt my chances at custody?

If custody is disputed, talk with your attorney about your plans to begin dating. Your dating may be irrelevant if the children are unaware of it. Most judges, however, will frown upon exposing your children to a new relationship when they are still adjusting to the separation of their parents. If your spouse is contesting custody, you may see that it would be best to focus your energy on your children, the litigation, and taking care of yourself.

If you do date and become sexually involved with your new partner, it is imperative that your children not be exposed to any sexual activity. If they are, it could harm your case for custody.

8.14 I'm gay and told my spouse that I was gay when I filed for divorce. What impact will my sexual orientation have on my case for custody or parenting time?

There have been North Carolina cases in the past that have allowed the court to treat being in a homosexual relationship negatively. In fact, at one time, gay marriage was banned in North Carolina. However, in 2015, the United States Supreme Court declared these types of laws unconstitutional. The right for gay individuals to marry is now the law of the land.

The trend appears to be that sexual orientation is becoming less and less significant to determining custody issues. Regardless of the social science research that concludes gay and lesbian parents are more similar than dissimilar to heterosexual parents, some judges continue to be critical toward homosexuality.

Be sure to choose a lawyer who you are confident will fully support you in your goals as a parent. Understand that, to dispel certain myths, you may need to "educate" your spouse, opposing counsel, and the judge.

8.15 How is *abandonment* legally defined, and how might it affect the outcome of our custody battle?

Under North Carolina law, *abandonment* is determined by the facts and circumstances of each case. It must have occurred for a period of six months or more and be without a just cause or excuse. The intentional absence of a parent's presence, care, protection, and support are all considered.

Abandonment, under certain circumstances, is considered a crime in North Carolina. Abandonment is not normally an issue in custody litigation unless one parent has been absent from the child's life for an extended period, although failing to spend time with your child without just cause will be a factor in determining that parent's parenting time.

Where abandonment has occurred for a period of six months or longer, a court may consider not only keeping the offending spouse from having custody, but also the court may actually terminate his or her parental rights if doing so would be in the best interest of the child.

8.16   Can I have witnesses speak on my behalf to try to get custody of my children?

Absolutely. Witnesses are critical in every custody case. At a temporary hearing, a witness is more likely to provide testimony by affidavit, which is a written, sworn statement. At a trial for the final determination of custody, you and the other parent will each have an opportunity to have witnesses give live testimony on your behalf. Among those you might consider as potential witnesses in your custody case are:

- Family members
- Family friends
- Parents of your children's friends
- Child-care providers
- Neighbors
- Coaches
- Teachers and tutors
- Health care providers
- Clergy members

In considering which witnesses would best support your case, your attorney may consider the following:

- What has been this witness's opportunity to observe you or the other parent, especially with your child? How frequently? How recently?
- How long has the witness known you or the other parent?
- What is the relationship of the witness to the child and the parents?
- How valuable is the knowledge that this witness has?
- Does this witness have knowledge different from that of other witnesses?

- Is the witness available and willing to testify?
- Is the witness clear in conveying information?
- Is the witness credible, that is, will the judge believe this witness?
- Does the witness have any biases or prejudices that could impact the testimony?

You and your attorney can work together to determine which witnesses will best support your case. Support your attorney by providing a list of potential witnesses together with your opinion regarding the answers to the above questions.

Give your attorney the phone numbers, addresses, and workplaces of each of your potential witnesses. This information can be critical for the role that the attorney has in interviewing the witnesses, contacting them regarding testifying, and issuing subpoenas to compel their court attendance if needed. When parents give conflicting testimony during a custody trial, the testimony of other witnesses can be key to determining the outcome of the case.

8.17 How old do the children have to be before they can speak to the judge about whom they want to live with?

It depends upon the judge. There is no set age at which children are allowed to speak to the judge about their preferences as to custody.

If either you or your spouse want to have the judge listen to what your child has to say, a request is ordinarily made to the judge to have the child speak to the judge in the judge's office (an *in camera* interview in the judges' chambers) rather than from the witness stand. Depending upon the judge's decision, the attorneys for you and your spouse may also be present.

It is possible that the judge may also allow the attorneys to question the child. Typically, the testimony of the child is made "on the record," that is, in the presence of a court reporter. This is so that the testimony can be transcribed later in the event of an appeal. If you have concern about the other parent learning what your child says to the judge, you may want to see if the judge will speak to your child alone off the record.

In addition to the age of a child, a judge may consider such factors as the child's maturity and personality in determining whether an *in camera* interview of the child by the judge will be helpful to the custody decision-making process.

8.18   Will my attorney want to speak with my children?

In most cases your attorney will not ask to speak with your children. An exception might be where either parent has made allegations of abuse or neglect.

Not all attorneys are trained in appropriate interviewing techniques for children, especially for younger children. If the attorney has not spent a lot of time with children or is not familiar with child development, the interview may not provide meaningful information. Do not hesitate to ask your attorney about his or her experience in working with children before you agree to an interview of your child.

If your attorney asks to meet with your child, provide some background information about your child first. Let your attorney know your child's personality, some of his or her interests, and any topics that might upset your child. This background will help the attorney exercise the care essential anytime a professional questions a child.

If you are concerned that going to your attorney's office for an interview will cause undue anxiety for your child, ask your attorney whether the interview can take place in a setting that would be more comfortable for your child. This might be a public place or your home.

8.19   What is a *guardian ad litem?* Why is one appointed?

As mentioned earlier, a *guardian ad litem* is an individual who is appointed by the court to represent the best interest of the child. The guardian *ad litem* (GAL), is typically an attorney, who is directed by the judge to conduct an investigation on the issue of custody.

The guardian *ad litem* may be called as a witness by you or your spouse to give testimony of her or his knowledge, based upon the investigation. For example, he or she might testify regarding the unsafe housing conditions of a parent. In some cases, the attorneys may agree that a written report prepared by the guardian *ad litem* be received into evidence for the judge's consideration. A guardian *ad litem* is not appointed in every case and is typically appointed either by consent of the parents or when the court believes there is some danger facing the child.

8.20 How might a video of my child help my custody case?

A video of your child's day-to-day life can help the judge learn more about your child's needs. It can demonstrate how your child interacts with you, siblings, and other important people in your family's life. The judge can see your child's room, home, and neighborhood.

Talk to your lawyer about whether a video would be helpful in your case. Such a video should show routines in your child's day, including challenging moments such as bedtime or disciplining.

If your lawyer recommends making a video, talk with him or her about what scenes to include, the length of the video, keeping the original, and the editing process.

Videos of your and your spouse's interactions with your child can be very helpful to show what actually occurs in your house. Gathering family videos or taping what occurs in your presence can also be helpful to show interactions with your child. Prior to taping anyone else you need to seek legal advice about your authority to do so and whether is it will ultimately help your case or harm it. For instance, following your spouse around taking videos in front of your child may cause your child stress. This could later be worse than whatever you catch on video. Secretly videoing or recording people's conversations is permitted in certain circumstances, but also can be against various state and federal laws. It is best to develop a plan with your attorney and only pursue these options after a thorough discussion of whether and how this should be done.

8.21 Why might I not be awarded custody?

You will not be awarded custody if the judge determines that you are not fit to be a custodial parent. You may also not be awarded custody in the event the judge determines that, although you are fit to be awarded custody, it is in your child's best interest that custody is awarded to the other parent.

Determinations of your fitness to be a custodial parent and of the best interest of your child will largely depend upon the facts of your case. Reasons why a parent might be found to be unfit include a history of physical abuse, abandonment of the child, alcohol or drug abuse, or mental health problems that affect the ability to parent. A judge's ruling on the best interest of a child is based upon numerous factors.

A decision by the judge that your spouse should have custody does not require a conclusion that you are an unfit parent. Even if the judge determines that both you and your spouse are fit to have custody, he or she may nevertheless decide that it is in the best interest of your child that only one of you be awarded custody.

8.22   Does joint custody always mean equal time at each parent's house?

No. Joint custody does not necessarily mean an equal division of parenting time, nor does it require that the child "flip-flop" every other week between two homes. In North Carolina, joint physical custody is defined as both parents having at least one-third of the overnights in a year. This includes splitting custodial time equally or many other permeations of parenting times.

Joint legal custody describes the situation in which the parents share equally in the long-term decision making for your child. It can also be helpful to remember that day-to-day decisions, such as a child's daily routine, will usually be made by the parent who has the child that day.

Whether it is sole or joint custody, you and your spouse can agree to share parenting time in a way that best serves your children. An example would be one in which you and your spouse agree to joint legal custody, but where you will have physical custody with your child residing primarily with you.

8.23   What are some of the risks of joint custody?

Joint legal and/or joint physical custody may be a good idea when: the parents agree to it; the parents have been separated for a period of time and have been able to reach decisions regarding their children without the involvement of attorneys or the court; and when the other factors for joint custody are present.

Joint custody requires healthy communication between you and your spouse. Without it, you are at risk for conflict, stress, and delay when making important decisions for your child. If communication with your spouse regarding your child is poor, think carefully before agreeing to joint legal custody.

If you share joint legal custody and are unable to reach agreement on a major decision, such as a child's school or child-care provider, you and your former spouse may be required to return to mediation or to court to resolve your dispute. This can lead to delays in decision making for matters important to your child, increased conflict, and legal fees.

8.24   If my spouse is awarded physical custody of my child, how much time will our child spend with me?

Parenting time schedules for noncustodial parents vary from case to case. As in the determination of custody, the best interest of the child are what a court considers in determining the parenting time schedule. Among the factors that can impact a parenting time schedule are the past history of parenting time, the age and needs of the child, and the parents' work schedules.

If you and your spouse are willing to reach your own agreement about the parenting time schedule, you are likely to be more satisfied with it than with a schedule imposed by a judge. Because the two of you know your child's needs, your family traditions, and your personal preferences, you can design a plan uniquely suited to your child's best interest.

If you and your spouse are unable to reach an agreement on a parenting time schedule, the judge will decide the schedule. Judges vary wildly in their approaches to parenting time throughout the state and even within judicial districts.

8.25   What is a *parenting plan?*

A *parenting plan* is a document that details how you and your spouse will be parenting your child after the divorce. Parenting plans are typically developed through the court-ordered mediation process. These plans are then incorporated into a child-custody court order by your attorneys. Among the issues addressed in a parenting plan are:

- Custody, both legal and physical
- Parenting time, including specific times for regular school year, holidays, birthdays, Mother's Day and Father's Day, summer, and school breaks
- Phone access to the child
- Communication regarding the child
- Access to records regarding the child
- Notice regarding parenting time
- Attendance at the child's activities
- Decision making regarding the child
- Exchange of information such as addresses, phone numbers, and care providers

8.26 I don't think it's safe for my children to have any contact with my spouse. How can I prove this to the judge?

Keeping your children safe is so important that this discussion with your attorney requires immediate attention. Talk with your attorney about a plan for the protection of you and your children. Options might include a protective order, supervised visitation, or certain restrictions on your spouse's parenting time.

Make sure you have an attorney who understands your concerns for the welfare of your children. If your attorney is not taking your worry about the safety of your children seriously, you may be better served by a lawyer with a greater understanding of the issues in your case.

Give your attorney a complete history of the facts upon which you base your belief that your children are not safe with the other parent. While the most recent facts and incidents are often the most relevant, it is important that your attorney have a clear picture of the background as well.

Your attorney also needs information about your spouse, such as whether your spouse is or has been:

- Using alcohol or drugs
- Treated for alcohol or drug use

- Arrested, charged, or convicted of crimes of violence
- In possession of firearms
- Subject to a protective order for harassment or violence

8.27 My spouse keeps saying he'll get custody because there were no witnesses to his abuse and I can't prove it. Is he right?

No. Most domestic violence is not witnessed by others, and judges know this. This is a threat used by many abusive spouses to maintain control over their victims. If you have been a victim of abusive behavior by your spouse, or if you have witnessed your children as victims, your testimony is likely to be the most compelling evidence.

Be sure to tell your attorney about anyone who may have either seen your spouse's behavior or spoken to you or your children right after an abusive incident. They may be important witnesses in your custody case.

8.28 I am concerned about protecting my child from abuse by my spouse. Which types of past abuse by my spouse are important to tell my attorney?

Keeping your child safe is your top priority. So that your attorney can help you protect your child, give him or her a full history of the following:

- Hitting, kicking, pushing, shoving, or slapping you or your child
- Sexual abuse
- Threats harm to you or the child
- Threats to abduct your child
- Destruction of property
- Torture or other harm to pets
- Requiring your child to keep secrets
- Limiting your or your child's access to communicate to others about the abuse
- Isolating you or your child from friends and family

The process of writing down past events may help you to remember other incidents of abuse that you had forgotten. Be as complete as possible.

8.29 What documents or items should I give my attorney to help prove the history of domestic violence by my spouse?

The following may be useful exhibits if your case goes to court:

- Photographs of injuries
- Photographs of damaged property
- Abusive or threatening notes, letters, texts, or e-mails
- Abusive or threatening voice messages
- Videos or audio of your spouse abusing or threatening you (speak with an attorney prior to secretly recording anyone without their permission, as it is allowed, only in certain circumstances)
- Your journal entries about abuse
- Police reports
- Medical records
- Court records
- Criminal and traffic records
- Your spouse's psychological records
- Damaged property, such as torn clothing
- Weapons used in the act of domestic violence

Discuss with your attorney any of these that you are able to obtain and ask your lawyer whether others can be acquired through a subpoena or other means.

8.30 How can I get the other parent's visitation to be supervised?

If you are concerned about the safety of your children when they are with the other parent, talk to your lawyer. It may be that a protection order is warranted to terminate or limit contact with your children. Alternatively, it is possible to ask the judge to consider certain court orders intended to better protect your children.

Ask your attorney whether, under the facts of your case, the judge would consider any of the following court orders:

- Supervised visits
- Exchanges of the children in a public place

- Parenting class for the other parent
- Anger management or other rehabilitative program for the other parent
- A prohibition against drinking or other substance usage by the other parent when with the children

Judges have differing approaches to cases where children are at risk. Recognize that there are also often practical considerations, such as cost or the availability of people to supervise visits. Urge your attorney to advocate zealously for court orders to protect your children from harm by the other parent.

8.31 I want to talk to my spouse about our child, but all she wants to do is argue. How can I communicate without it always turning into a fight?

Because conflict is high between you and your spouse, consider the following:

- Ask your lawyer to help you obtain a court order for custody and parenting time that is specific and detailed. This lowers the amount of necessary communication between you and your spouse. You may want to ask the court to appoint a parent coordinator (PC) to assist you in your communications and decision making.
- Put as much information in writing as possible. Consider using e-mail, text, mail, or fax, especially for less urgent communication.
- Avoid criticisms of your spouse's parenting.
- Avoid directing your spouse regarding how to parent.
- Be factual, concise, and business-like.
- Acknowledge to your spouse the good parental qualities she displays, such as being concerned, attentive, or generous.
- Keep your child out of any conflicts.

By focusing on your behavior, conflict with your spouse has the potential to decrease.

8.32 What is a *parent coordinator?*

A *parent coordinator (PC)* is a neutral third party appointed in a high-conflict child-custody case to assist parents in reducing the conflicts that arise from day-to-day decision making. The PC identifies disputed issues, reduces misunderstandings, clarifies the priorities of the parents, explores possibilities for compromise, develops methods of collaboration in parenting, and helps the parties comply with the court's order of custody.

A PC can be an experienced and credentialed counselor or a lawyer who has completed a training protocol in parent coordinating. A PC focuses on solutions that benefit the minor child and minimize or reduce the conflict between the parents. Although the PC cannot decide who ultimately will have primary custody, they do facilitate and potentially decide other day-to-day issues as specified in the court order. The PC is a stopgap measure between court orders. Although they are typically appointed in the permanent custody order, judges occasionally utilize parenting coordinators during the litigation process.

8.33   What is a *high-conflict case?*

A *high-conflict case* is defined in North Carolina as a custody case in which there has been an ongoing pattern of any of the following: excessive litigation, anger and distrust between the parents, verbal abuse, physical aggression or threats of physical aggression, and difficulty communicating about the care of the child. Many times, high-conflict cases involve parents who try to win at all costs rather do what is best for their child.

8.34   What if the child is not returned from parenting time at the agreed-upon time? Should I call the police?

Calling the police should be done only as a last resort if you feel that your child is at risk for abuse or neglect, or if you have been advised by your attorney that such a call is warranted. The involvement of law enforcement officials in parental conflict can result in far greater trauma to a child than a late return at the end of a parenting time. If there is no court order in place it is likely that the police will not get involved in resolving this dispute, unless your child is in danger. Further, if calling the police causes your child stress and trauma, it could actually hinder the ultimate resolution of your custody dispute.

The appropriate response to a child not being returned according to a court order depends upon the circumstances. If the problem is a recurring one, talk to your attorney regarding your options. You may seek to have the court admonish the other parent or hold her in contempt. It may be that a corresponding change in the schedule would be in the best interest of your child.

Regardless of the behavior of the other parent, make every effort to keep your child out of any conflicts between the adults.

8.35   If I have full custody, may I move out of state without the permission of the court?

Not necessarily. It will depend on the language in your order and whether or not the move will frustrate the parenting time or rights of the other parent. If there are no restrictions on the order you may be allowed to move initially, but then your former spouse could potentially ask for the original order to be modified. If your former spouse agrees to your move, contact your attorney to prepare and submit the necessary documents to your former spouse and the court for approval. If your former spouse objects to your move and applies to the court for a modification, the court will have a hearing for the judge to decide whether or not there has been a substantial change in circumstance affecting your child.

If the judge believes there has been a substantial change in circumstance affecting your child, you will now need to prove that the move is in the best interest of your child. This means you will need to prove that the move will benefit your child. Some factors the court will consider are: your motives for moving; your former spouse's motives for objecting to the move; whether you will likely comply with the custody order; your ability to have a realistic parenting schedule that will preserve and foster the relationship of your child with your former spouse; and whether the minor child will benefit from the move. Therefore, it is helpful to have a legitimate reason for the move.

Examples of legitimate reasons for your move may include: removing the child from a dangerous peer group, or you are being transferred or have the opportunity for a better job that will allow your child to have a better standard of living. The court will consider strongly how the move will affect the parenting plan that is in place and the relationship the minor child has with the other parent. It is important to begin your case as soon as possible, so you will have time to get a final court ruling determining whether you may move out of state with your child prior to your move. You do not want to have already moved and then have the judge require that the child move back. This would provide unnecessary disruption to both your life and your child's life.

8.36 When ruling on whether to allow you to move out of state, what types of factors demonstrate the best interest of the child?

In determining your child's best interest, the court may consider many factors. These can include your child's ties to North Carolina, the quality of the community you want to move to, or your child's relationship with the other parent. If you are considering an out-of-state move, talk to your attorney immediately. Do so even if you have not finalized your plans. There are important facts for you to gather as soon as possible about potential housing, school, and day care.

8.37 After the divorce, can my spouse legally take our children out of the state during parenting time? Out of the country?

It depends upon the terms of the court order. If you are concerned about your children being out of North Carolina with the other parent, discuss the possibility of some of these court order provisions regarding out-of-state travel with your child:

- Limits on the duration or distance for out-of-state travel with the child
- Notice requirements
- Information on phone numbers
- Information on physical addresses
- E-mail address contact information
- Possession of the child's passport with either parent or a third party

- Posting of bond by the other parent prior to travel
- Requiring a court order for travel outside of the country

Although judges are not ordinarily concerned about short trips across state lines, you should let your attorney know if you are concerned that your child may be abducted by the other parent so that reasonable safeguards may be put in place.

8.38 If I am not given custody, what rights do I have regarding medical records and medical treatment for my child?

Regardless of which parent has custody, the law allows both parents to have access to the medical records of their children and to make emergency medical decisions, unless otherwise specifically restricted in a court order.

8.39 If I'm not the primary caregiver, how will I know what's going on at my child's school? What rights to records do I have there?

Regardless of your custodial status, you have a legal right to access your child's school records unless otherwise specifically restricted in a court order.

More important than the written records is being involved in your child's school. Develop a relationship with your child's teachers and the school staff. Request to be put on the school's mailing list for all notices. Sign up for online resources where you can learn about your child's progress such as your child's teacher's web or wiki page, or accessing your parent portal through "PowerSchool." Find out what is necessary for you to get copies of important school information and report cards.

Communicate with the other parent to both share and receive information about your child's progress in school. This will enable you to support your child and one another through any challenging periods of your child's education. It also enables you to share a mutual pride in your child's successes.

Regardless of which parent has custody, your child will benefit by your involvement in his or her education by your participation in parent-teacher conferences, attendance at open houses and other school events, help with school homework, and positive communication with the other parent.

8.40 What if my child does not want to go for scheduled parenting time? Can my former spouse force the child to go?

If your child is resisting spending time with the other parent, it can first be helpful to determine the underlying reason. Consider these questions:

- What is your child's stated reason for not wanting to go?
- Does your child appear afraid, anxious, or sad?
- Do you have any concerns regarding your child's safety while with the other parent?
- Have you prepared your child for being with the other parent, speaking about the experience with enthusiasm and encouragement?
- Is it possible your child is perceiving your anxiety about the situation and is consequently having the same reaction?
- Have you provided support for your child's transition to the other home, such as completing fun activities in your home well in advance of the other parent's starting time for parenting?
- Have you spoken to the other parent about your child's behavior?
- Can you provide anything that will make your child's time with the other parent more comfortable, such as a favorite toy or blanket?
- Have you established clear routines that support your child to be ready to go with the other parent with ease, such as packing a backpack or saying good-bye to a family pet?

The reason for a child's reluctance to go with the other parent may be as simple as being sad about leaving you or as serious as being a victim of abuse in the other parent's home. It is important to look at this closely to determine the best response.

Judges treat compliance with court orders for parenting time seriously. If one parent believes that the other is intentionally interfering with parenting time or the parent-child relationship, it can result in further litigation. At the same time, you want to know that your child is safe. Talk with your attorney about the best approach in your situation.

8.41 What steps can I take to prevent my spouse from getting the children in the event of my death?

Unless the other parent is not fit to have custody, he or she will have first priority as the guardian of your child in the event of your death.

All parents should have a will naming a guardian for their children. Talk with your attorney and get a referral for an experienced estate-planning attorney to draft a will for you. Further, seek counsel about how to best document and preserve the evidence that will be needed to prove that the other parent is unfit to have custody in the event of your death.

9

Child Support

Whether you will be paying child support or receiving it, child support is often the subject of much worry. Will I receive enough support to take care of my children? Will I have enough money to live on after I pay my child support? How will I make ends meet?

Most parents want to provide for their children. Today, the child-support laws make it possible for parents to have a better understanding of their obligation to support their children. The mechanisms for both payment and receipt of child support are more clearly defined, and help is available for collecting support if it is not paid.

The *North Carolina Child Support Guidelines,* and *North Carolina Child Support Enforcement* all help to simplify the child-support system. As you learn more about them, matters regarding child support that appear complex in the beginning can eventually become routine for you and the other parent.

9.1   What determines whether I will get child support?

Whether you will receive child support depends upon a number of factors. These may include: how much time your child is living in your household; which parent has custody; and the incomes of the parents and each parent's ability to pay support. If paying child support will cause your spouse to reduce his or her net income below the federal poverty guideline, the support you receive may be as little as $50 per month.

If you have physical custody of your child, it is likely your spouse will be ordered to pay support for any children born or adopted by you and your spouse during your marriage. Even in most joint physical custody arrangements you will likely receive child support if your spouse's income is significantly more than yours.

9.2 Can I request child support even if I do not meet the six-month residency requirement for a divorce in North Carolina?

Yes. Even though you may not meet the requirements to obtain a divorce, you have a right to seek support for your children. Talk to your attorney or visit the North Carolina Health and Human Services System's website at www.ncchildsupport. com for more information.

9.3 Can I get temporary support while waiting for custody to be decided?

A judge has authority to enter a temporary order for custody and/or child support. This order ordinarily remains in place until a final judgment establishing custody is decided. In most cases a hearing for temporary support can be held shortly after the filing of the complaint for child support.

9.4 What is *temporary support* and how soon can I get it?

Temporary support is money paid by one spouse to the other for the support of a spouse or a child. It is paid sometime after the divorce petition is filed and continues until a permanent child-support order is entered by the court or until your case is dismissed.

If you are in need of temporary support, talk to your attorney at your first opportunity. If you and your spouse are unable to agree upon the amount of temporary spousal or child support to be paid each month, talk to your attorney. If an agreement is not reached, it is likely that your attorney will file a motion for temporary support asking the judge to decide how much the support should be and when it will start.

Because there are a number of steps to getting a temporary child-support order, do not delay in discussing your need for support with your lawyer.

The following are the common steps in the process of obtaining support:

- You discuss your need for a temporary child-support order with your lawyer.
- You request an exchange of income information and expense information with your spouse.
- You try to resolve the matter prior to filing a claim.
- Your lawyer requests a hearing date from the judge and prepares the necessary documents.
- In most judicial districts you exchange a required *financial affidavit* and income documentation.
- A temporary hearing is held.
- The temporary order is signed by the judge.
- Your spouse begins paying child support to the North Carolina Child Support Centralized Collections (NCC-SCC) in Raleigh or you have his wages withheld and sent to NCCSCC.
- NCCSCC sends the money to you.

If your spouse is not paying you support voluntarily, time is of the essence in obtaining a temporary order for support. This should be one of the first issues you discuss with your lawyer.

9.5   How soon does my spouse have to start paying support for the children?

Your spouse may begin paying you support voluntarily at any time. A temporary order for support will give you the right to collect the support if your spouse stops paying. Talk to your lawyer about court hearings for temporary support in your county. You may have to wait for several weeks to several months before your temporary hearing can be held.

It is possible that the judge will not order child support to start until the first of the following month. The judge can also require that your spouse pay back the child-support arrears, the money he should have been paying you prior to the hearing. Typically, arrears are not paid back immediately and a payment plan is made for your spouse to pay you back over time.

9.6 How is the amount of child support I'll receive or pay figured?

The *North Carolina Child Support Guidelines* were created by the North Carolina conference of chief district court judges to develop the standards by which your child support is calculated. These guidelines are revised at least every four years to reflect cost-of-living increases. According to the guidelines, both parents have a duty to contribute to the support of their children in proportion to their respective net incomes. As a result, both your income and the income of your spouse will factor into the child-support calculation.

Other factors the court may consider include:

- The additional cost of health insurance for the child
- Extraordinary expenses for the child including travel expenses related to visitation
- Work-related child-care expenses
- Regularly paid support for other children
- Which parent claims the children as exemptions for tax purposes
- Additional money received outside of your employment or your spouse's employment, including gifts from friends or family

Child support may be determined on the child's actual needs and expenses instead of using the *North Carolina Child Support Guidelines* in certain cases. For example:

- When the parent's combined incomes exceed the limit of the guidelines, which is $30,000 per month
- When either parent or child has extraordinary medical costs
- When a child is disabled with special needs
- Whenever the application of the guidelines in an individual case would be unjust or inappropriate

When a judge orders an amount of support that is different from the guidelines amount, it is referred to as a "deviation." Due to the complexity of calculations under the guidelines, many attorneys use computer software to calculate child support. You can review the guidelines in greater detail at https://nddhacts01.dhhs.state.nc.us/WorkSheet.jsp.

9.7 Will the type of custody arrangement or the amount of parenting time I have impact the amount of child support I receive?

It can. Sharing joint physical custody can lower direct child-support amounts, but there is a requirement to share in the other expenses of your child. It is essential that you discuss child support with your attorney prior to reaching any agreements with your spouse regarding custody or parenting time. If you intend to mediate custody or parenting time, be sure to talk with your attorney in advance regarding how this can affect your child support.

9.8 Is overtime pay considered in the calculation of child support?

Yes, if your overtime is a regular part of your employment and you can actually expect to earn overtime regularly. The judge can consider your work history, the degree of control you have over your overtime, and the nature of the field in which you work.

9.9 Will rental income be factored into my child support, or just my salary?

Yes. Income from other sources such as rental income may be considered in determining the amount of child support.

9.10 My spouse has a college degree, but refuses to get a job. Will the court consider this in determining the amount of child support?

The earning capacity of your spouse may be considered instead of current income. The court can look at your spouse's recent work history, education, skills, health, and job opportunities. If you believe your spouse is earning substantially less than the income he or she is capable of earning, provide your attorney with details. Ask about making a case for child support based on earning capacity instead of actual income.

9.11 Will I get the child support directly from my spouse or from the state?

North Carolina law allows for child support to be paid directly from your spouse, if both parties agree to that arrangement. Otherwise, child support is paid through North Carolina Child Support Centralized Collections (NCCSCC) or withheld from the income of the payor of child support. Employers routinely withhold child support from employee wages just as they withhold taxes or retirement.

If the parent's income is not being withheld by an employer, the parent either makes child-support payments directly if both parents agree or through NCCSCC. Payments can be made by check or money order through the mail. NCCSCC then sends the child support to the parent receiving support via direct deposit or debit card.

9.12 If my spouse sends in a child-support payment to the state, how quickly will the state get me the money?

A number of factors that affect how quickly your child-support payment will be paid to you after it is received by NCCSCC, such as whether it is an out-of-state check or a certified check. NCCSCC will give you your child support by direct deposit or through a debit card. More information can be found on the North Carolina Child Support Enforcement website at www2.ncdhhs.gov/dss/cse/docs/csehandbook.pdf.

9.13 Is there any reason not to pay or receive payments directly to or from my spouse once the court has entered a child-support order?

Yes. Once a child-support order is entered by the court, the NCCSCC keeps a record of all support paid through centralized collections. If the payment is not made through centralized collections, the state's records will not show whether the paying parent is behind in his or her child-support payments.

Direct payments of child support can also result in misunderstandings between parents. The payor may have intended the money to pay a child-support payment, but the parent receiving the support may have thought it was extra money to help with the child's expenses. The payment of support through the centralized collections protects both parents and reduces conflicts.

9.14 How soon can I expect my child-support payments to start arriving?

A number of factors may affect the date on which you will begin receiving your child support. The usual steps in the process are:

- A child-support amount and start date for the support is decided either by agreement between you and your spouse or by the judge.
- Either your attorney or your spouse's attorney prepares the court order.
- The attorney who did not write the court order reviews and approves it.
- The court order is taken to the judge for signature.
- If wages are to be withheld, your spouse signs a *notice to withhold income* form and delivers it to his or her employer, asking that child support be withheld from future paychecks.
- Your spouse's employer withholds the support from the paycheck.
- The child support is transferred by the employer into the North Carolina Child Support Centralized Collections (NCCSCC).
- If your spouse is paying through centralized collections, he submits his payments to them directly.
- The NCCSCC then sends the money to you by direct deposit or by debit card.
- If you choose to have direct payments, you will receive them directly from your spouse when he or she sends the payments to you.

As you can see, there are a lot of steps in this process. Plan your budget knowing that the initial payment of child support may be delayed.

9.15 Will some amount of child support be withheld from every paycheck?

It depends upon the employer's policy and how you are paid. If support is due on the first of the month, the employer has the full month to withhold the amount ordered to be paid.

If an employer issues paychecks twice a month, it is possible that half of the support will be withheld from each check and paid in to the NCCSCC at the end of the month.

If an employer issues checks every other week, which is twenty-six pay periods per year, there will be some months in which a third paycheck is issued. Consequently, it is possible that no child support will be withheld from the wages paid in that third check of the month, or that some checks will be for less than 50 percent of the monthly amount due. Over time, child-support payments typically fall into a routine schedule which makes it easier for both the payor and the recipient of support to plan their budgets.

9.16 If my spouse has income other than from an employer, is it still possible to get a court order to withhold my child support from his income?

Yes. Child support can be automatically withheld from a most sources of income. These may include unemployment, worker's compensation, retirement plans, and investment income.

9.17 The person I am divorcing is not the biological parent of my child. Can I still collect child support from my spouse?

Perhaps. Your spouse is presumed to be the father of all children born during your marriage, unless it can be proven otherwise. So he will likely be considered the biological father of your child unless a paternity test indicates he is not. Your spouse may be ordered to pay child support under certain other circumstances as well.

Discuss the facts of your case with your lawyer in detail. When you are clear about what will be in the best interest of your child, your attorney can support you in developing a strategy for your case that takes into consideration not only child support but also the future relationship of your spouse with your child.

9.18 Can I collect child support from both the biological parent and the adoptive parent of my child?

When your child was adopted, the biological parent's rights and obligations to your child ended, including the biological parent's obligation to continue paying child support.

9.19 What happens with child support when our children go to the other parent's home for summer vacation? Is child support still due?

Yes, it is still due, but it will depend on the specifics of your custody order. Child support is typically based on the amount of overnights throughout the year and not based on summertime visitation schedules. This means that you may need to save some of the money from the summer visit to provide for your child's needs during the school year or vice versa.

9.20 After the divorce, if I choose to live with my new partner rather than marry, can I still collect child support?

Yes. Although spousal support (alimony) may end if you live with your partner, child support does not terminate for this reason.

9.21 Can I still collect child support if I move to another state?

Yes. A move out of state will not end your right to receive child support. However, the amount of child support could be changed if other circumstances change, such as income, work-related child-care costs, or costs for exercising parenting time.

9.22 Can I expect to continue to receive child support if I remarry?

Yes. You will continue to receive child support even if you remarry.

9.23 How long can I expect to receive child support?

Under North Carolina law, child support is ordinarily ordered to be paid until the child dies, marries, is emancipated (becomes self-supporting), or reaches the age of eighteen. However, child support continues after a child's eighteenth birthday if he or she is still making progress toward graduating from high school and is not yet twenty. Of course, you or your spouse can agree by contract to pay child support longer than otherwise required by law.

9.24   Can we resolve our claims by a private agreement?

Yes. North Carolina law allows parents to enter into private child-support agreements, and the courts will enforce these agreements as long as it is for the best interest of the minor child. Sometimes it is better to enter into a private agreement to ensure provisions that exceed the requirements of North Carolina law. Some examples include: extending child support beyond age eighteen; or requiring payment of college tuition, which could be modified if included in a court order. It is important to have an in-depth conversation with your attorney to determine whether a private agreement or a court order is best for you.

9.25   How is enforcing a *child-support agreement* different from enforcing a *child-support order?*

You must enforce a child-support agreement yourself by starting a whole new lawsuit when your spouse fails to live up to his or her obligations in the agreement. A judge, however, enforces a child-support order and, when asked, can quickly punish (with fines and even jail) someone who fails to follow the court's order. Getting into court on a motion for contempt is much faster typically then starting a new case to enforce an agreement.

9.26   Can my agreement or order by modified?

Either an agreement or an order can be modified. The order is typically easier to modify than an agreement. In either case a substantial change in circumstance has to occur for modification to be allowed. The simple passage of three years in time and an increase in the amount due under the child-support guidelines could be sufficient to modify an order. To change an agreement, you will need to show that the needs and expenses and/or the relative abilities to pay for those needs have changed. This usually requires a more detailed financial affidavit and financial documentation.

9.27 What can I do if my former spouse refuses to pay my court-ordered child support?

If your former spouse is not paying child support, you may take action to enforce your court order either with the help of your lawyer or the assistance of a *child-support attorney*. Unlike a private attorney, you do not pay for the services of a child support attorney.

Visit the website for the North Carolina Health and Human Services System at www.ncdhhs.gov/assistance/childrens-services/child-support-enforcement for a listing of the offices and addresses of child-support attorneys who can help you.

Most counties have attorneys who are specifically designated to perform child-support enforcement services. These attorneys are sometimes referred to as *child-support enforcement attorneys*. The judge may order payment of both the current amount of support and an additional amount to be paid each month until the past-due child support (referred to as "arrearages") is paid in full.

You may request that your former spouse's state and federal tax refunds be sent directly to the North Carolina Child Support Centralized Collections. It may also be possible to garnish a checking or savings account for past-due child support.

State-issued licenses (for example, driver's, hunting, and fishing licenses) may also be suspended if a parent falls behind in child-support payments. Your former spouse may also be found in contempt of court if the failure to pay support is intentional. Possible consequences include being fined, paying your attorney's fees, being censured, or being jailed.

To review, if you are not receiving child support, you have three options:

- Call you attorney.
- Call your local Child Support Enforcement Office.
- Visit the North Carolina Health and Human Services at www.ncdhhs.gov/assistance/childrens-services/child-support-enforcement.

9.28   At what point will the state help me collect back child support, and what methods do they use?

It depends. When the state will help you collect past-due child support and the methods it will use can depend upon the amount of past due child support owed.

Driver's, recreational, and professional licenses can be suspended if the equivalent of more than one month of child support is owed. If more than $500 in back support is past due, state or federal income tax refunds can be intercepted. In cases in which more than $2,500 is owed, a passport can be denied. In some cases, failure to pay child support can result in a jail sentence. You must initiate contact with the state if you want help in collecting your child support.

9.29   I live outside of North Carolina. Will the money I spend on airline tickets to see my children impact my child support?

It might. If you expect to spend large sums of money for transportation in order to have parenting time with your children, talk to your attorney about how this might be taken into consideration as an extraordinary expense when determining the amount of child support.

9.30   After the divorce, can my former spouse substitute buying sprees with the child for child-support payments?

No. Purchases of gifts and clothing for a child do not relieve your former spouse from an obligation to pay you child support.

9.31   Are expenses such as child care and health insurance supposed to be included in my child support?

Yes. Child-care expenses are entered into a separate row in the child-support work sheet, because the North Carolina Child Support Guidelines recognize that child care varies greatly, depending on the age of the child and the location of the child care. This expense as well as medical insurance will increase or decrease the baseline of child-support expenses depending on who pays these expenses. The person who pays these expenses will be credited for a portion of this expense in the determination of child support.

Other expenses for your child such as clothing, school lunches, and the cost for activities are ordinarily paid for by you if you are receiving child support according to the guidelines, unless the court order in your case provides otherwise.

9.32 Can my spouse be required by the court to pay for our child's private elementary and high school education?

Sometimes. The *North Carolina Child Support Guidelines* adjust for private school if it is considered an extraordinary expense. Also, you can ask that the court deviate from the guidelines to require a parent who has been paying for private school to continue to do so. It is more difficult to convince the court to provide for private school if the child is not currently enrolled in private school unless the child has a particular individual need that cannot be provided for in public school. Some parents agree to include a provision in the court order for payment of such tuition because both parents believe it is important for their child.

If you want your spouse to share this expense for your child, talk it over with your lawyer. Be sure to provide your attorney with information regarding tuition, fees, and other expenses related to private education.

9.33 Can my spouse be required by the court to contribute financially to our child's college education?

The legal duty of a parent to support a child does not include payment for college education. However, if your spouse agrees to pay this expense, you may want to include this in a private child-support agreement. If your agreement includes a provision for payment of college education expenses, be sure it is specific. Terms to consider include:

- Which expenses are included? For example: tuition, room and board, books, fees, and travel fees.
- Will the cost be paid by only one parent, split equally, or in some other proportional way?
- Is there a limit? For example, does the agreement include an amount up to the level of the published cost

of attendance at the University of North Carolina at Chapel Hill or a certain dollar amount?

- When is payment due?
- For what period of time does payment continue?
- Are there any limits on the type of education that will be paid for?
- Will you set requirements for your child to maintain a certain minimal grade point average (GPA)?
- Is this provision modifiable?

The greater the clarity in such a provision, the lower the risk is for misunderstanding or conflict years later.

10

Alimony

The mere mention of the word "alimony" might stir your emotions and start your stomach churning. If your spouse filed for divorce and sought alimony, you might see it as is a double injustice—your marriage is ending and you feel like you have to pay for it, too. If you are seeking spousal support, you might feel hurt and confused that your spouse is resistant to helping to support you, even though you interrupted your career to stay home and care for your children.

Learning more about North Carolina's laws on alimony, also referred to as *spousal support,* can help you move from your emotional reaction to it to the reality of possible outcomes in your case. Uncertainty about the precise amount of alimony that may be awarded or the number of years it might be paid is not unusual. Work closely with your lawyer. Be open to possibilities. Try looking at it from your spouse's perspective.

With the help of your lawyer, you will know the best course of action to take toward an alimony decision you can live with after your divorce is over.

10.1 Which gets calculated first, child support or alimony?

Typically, temporary child support is determined at the same time as temporary alimony, which is called *post-separation support (PSS)*. More often than not, alimony is the last issue resolved after permanent child support is determined and the property issues have been resolved.

10.2 What's the difference between *spousal support* and *alimony*?

"Spousal support" includes alimony as well as post-separation support (PSS).

10.3 What is *post-separation support*?

Post-separation support or *PSS* is a temporary no-fault form of spousal support awarded from the date of separation until the entry of an alimony award or the dismissal of the alimony claim. PSS is based on your current needs in expenses in excess of your income and your spouse's current ability to pay.

10.4 Can my husband get spousal support?

Both wives and husbands can get spousal support under the right circumstances. The primary factors to determine this support involves answering the question: Who is the supporting spouse and who is the dependent spouse? The supporting spouse is basically the spouse who earns more money and would have income in excess of his or her expenses.

The dependent spouse is the one who does not have sufficient funds to cover his or her reasonable needs and expenses. In many families, neither spouse is able to be a supporting spouse and therefore spousal support is not awarded by the court. Likewise, if neither spouse is dependent on the other, then spousal support is not awarded.

10.5 What are *reasonable needs and expenses*?

Reasonable needs and expenses are based on your standard of living and your current living expenses. Oftentimes there are no longer sufficient funds to provide for luxuries from the marriage. A judge may feel that some of your expenses or those of your spouse are unreasonable. Before moving out of the marital home or creating a tight budget, you first should meet with an attorney. Your current needs may affect how much you pay or receive in PSS and/or alimony.

10.6 Are there different types of alimony?

There are several different types of alimony, including lump sum, rehabilitative or fixed-term, and lifetime. *Lump sum alimony* is a one-time payment of alimony that is frequently agreed to in settlements rather than one ordered by the court. You should use caution with lump sum alimony, as there are significant hidden possible tax consequences. Some judges may award alimony for a fixed period of time *(rehabilitative alimony)* to enable you or your spouse to obtain further training, or education, to be more able to support yourself. Rehabilitative alimony is the most common form of alimony in North Carolina. Less common is *lifetime alimony,* which terminates only upon your death, remarriage, or cohabitation with another partner.

10.7   How will I know if I am eligible to receive alimony?

Talk with your attorney about whether you are a candidate for alimony.

Judges vary greatly in their opinions about whether to award alimony. Among the factors that may affect your eligibility to receive alimony are:

- The length of your marriage
- Your contributions to the marriage, including the interruption of your career for the care of children or to support your spouse's career
- Whether your or your spouse's income will be impacted by being the custodial parent of the child
- Your and your spouse's education, work history, health, income, and earning capacity
- Your overall financial situation compared to that of your spouse
- Your need for support
- Your spouse's ability to pay support
- The ages, mental, emotional, and physical conditions of both spouses
- The relative assets and debts of the spouses, including marital and separate property
- Tax consequences
- Your standard of living during the marriage
- Marital misconduct by either spouse
- Any economic factor the judge finds to be just and proper to consider

Every case for alimony is unique and a judge will have broad discretion. Providing your lawyer with clear and detailed information about the facts of your marriage and current financial situation will increase the likelihood of a fair outcome for you.

10.8 What information should I provide to my attorney if I want alimony?

If your attorney advises you that you may be a candidate for alimony, be sure to provide complete facts about your situation, including:

- A history of the interruptions in your education or career for the benefit of your spouse, including transfers or moves due to your spouse's employment
- A history of the interruptions in your education or career for raising children, including periods during which you worked part-time
- Your complete educational background, including the dates of your schooling or training and degrees earned
- Your work history, including the names of your employers, the dates of your employment, your duties, your pay, and the reason you left
- Any pensions or other benefits lost due to the interruption of your career for the benefit of the marriage
- Your health history, including any current diagnoses, treatments, limitations, and medications
- Your monthly living expenses, including anticipated future expenses such as health insurance and tax on alimony
- A complete list of the assets and debts for you and your spouse
- Income for you and your spouse, including all sources
- Your recent joint tax returns, investment accounts, bank accounts, and credit card account statements

You also should include any other facts that might support your need for alimony, such as other contributions you made to the marriage, upcoming medical treatment, or a lack of jobs in the field in which you were formerly employed.

No two alimony cases are alike. The better the information your lawyer has about your situation, the easier it will be for him or her to assess your case for alimony.

10.9 What is *marital misconduct* and how does it affect my spousal support?

Marital misconduct includes many different behaviors that may have occurred during the marriage. This includes such things as: adultery, substance abuse, domestic violence, abandonment, indignities, maliciously throwing your spouse out, and cruel treatment.

Though marital misconduct is no longer necessary to obtain a divorce, it is still a factor for the determination of the amount or duration of alimony in North Carolina. The weight marital misconduct is given varies greatly from judge to judge.

Although marital misconduct can be brought up in a temporary spousal support hearing, many judges frequently do not rely on the misconduct to determine the amount or duration of temporary support. In both post-separation support (PSS) and alimony cases, the judge has a lot of discretion in how strongly to consider marital misconduct to the spousal support award.

10.10 My spouse told me that because I had an affair during the marriage, I have no chance to get alimony even though I quit my job and have cared for our children for many years. Is it true that I have no case?

Yes, an affair prior to your separation is a complete bar to alimony unless an exception applies. It is important to divulge information about an affair to your attorney so that he or she can develop a strategy on how to handle your situation.

If your spouse has also had an affair before you separated, then the court does not have to bar your alimony claim. If your spouse condoned or forgave your affair, you may still be entitled to alimony. Condoning an affair can be explicit (your spouse says "I forgive you") or implicit (having sexual relations with you, going through extensive counseling, and/or resuming the marital relationship after knowing you have had an affair). The key to condoning the affair is that your spouse has to know about the affair before he or she forgives you.

Lastly, having an affair is not an absolute bar to being awarded temporary spousal support such as post-separation support.

10.11   How is the amount of alimony calculated?

Unlike child support, there are no specific guidelines for determining the amount of alimony. A judge will look at the reasonable needs, expenses, and incomes of you and your spouse as well as the marital misconduct of you and your spouse. Judges are given wide discretion to determine alimony without being tied to specific guidelines. Consequently, the outcome of an alimony ruling by a judge can be one of the most unpredictable aspects of your divorce.

10.12   My spouse makes a lot more money than he reports on our tax return, but he hides it. How can I prove my spouse's real income to show he can afford to pay alimony?

Alert your attorney to your concerns. Your lawyer can then take a number of actions to determine your spouse's income with greater accuracy. This is likely to include:

- More thorough discovery
- An examination of check registers and bank deposits
- Reviewing purchases made in cash
- Inquiring about travel
- Depositions of third parties who have knowledge of income or spending by your spouse
- Subpoenas of records of places where your spouse has made large purchases or received income
- Comparing income claimed with expenses paid

By partnering with your lawyer, you may be able to build a case to establish your spouse's actual income as greater than what is shown on your tax returns. If you filed joint tax returns, discuss with your lawyer all other implications of erroneous information on those returns.

10.13 How is the purpose of alimony different from the payment of my property settlement?

Spousal support and the division of property serve two distinct purposes, even though many of the factors for determining them are the same. The purpose of alimony is to pay for your continued support, whereas the purpose of a property division is to distribute the marital assets fairly between you and your spouse.

10.14 How long can I expect to receive alimony?

The trend in North Carolina has been to move away from lifetime alimony awards. Like your right to receive alimony, the length of time you will receive alimony will depend upon the facts of your case and the judge's philosophy toward alimony. In general, the longer your marriage, the stronger your case is for a longer term of an alimony award.

If you are younger and/or have had a shorter-term marriage, you may receive only rehabilitative alimony for several years, while you attend school or get job training. Talk to your attorney about the facts of your case. Unless you and your spouse agree otherwise, your alimony will terminate upon the resumption of your marital relations with your spouse, the death of either spouse, or your remarriage or cohabitation.

10.15 Does remarriage affect my alimony?

Yes. Under North Carolina law, your alimony ends upon remarriage unless your agreement says otherwise.

10.16 Can I continue to collect alimony if I move to a different state?

Yes. The duty of your former spouse to follow a court order to pay alimony does not end simply because you move to another state, unless otherwise specified by the court order.

10.17 What can I do if my spouse stops paying alimony?

If your spouse stops paying alimony, see your attorney about your options for enforcing your court order. The judge may order the support to be taken from a source of your spouse's income, from a financial account belonging to your spouse, or through the sale or transfer of his property. The court could require your spouse to place a bond or give you a deed of trust/mortgage on his real property to secure the amounts your spouse owes.

If your spouse intentionally refuses to pay spousal support, talk to your attorney about pursuing a *contempt of court* action. In a contempt action, your spouse may be ordered to appear in court and provide evidence explaining why support has not been paid. Possible consequences for contempt of court include a jail sentence, payment of your attorney fees, or a fine.

10.18 Can I return to court to modify alimony?

It depends. If your agreement provides that your alimony order is "non-modifiable," then you may not have it modified. Also, if no award of alimony was made before or in the divorce decree and you do not have a claim for alimony pending, you will not be entitled to receive alimony in the future.

If there has been a "material change" in the circumstances of either you or your spouse, either spouse may seek to have alimony modified. Examples of a material change include a serious illness, losing a job, or obtaining a new job.

A complaint to modify alimony for the purposes of seeking additional alimony may not be filed if the time for payment of alimony allowed under your original alimony order has already passed. If you think you have a basis to modify your alimony, contact your attorney at once to be sure a timely modification request is filed with the court.

11

Division of Property

You likely picked out a house with your spouse with plans to raise your family together. You watched your children grow up in that house and created countless memories. Now, you find you may have to sell your home because you are getting a divorce. What will happen to all of your possessions? Who decides what you get to keep? Will you have to fight with your spouse over who gets cherished items?

Dividing your property during a divorce can be complicated. Some assets are simple to valuate while others can require a complex determination by an expert. Obtain your attorney's advice to help you decide which property can be easily divided and which property may require an expert's opinion. Your attorney can assist you in considering all of the factors in deciding which items to sell, which items to give to your spouse, and which items to keep for yourself.

Reaching an agreement with your spouse as to division of property can save you time and legal fees. When it comes to household items, try to work together with your spouse to decide how to split up your property. Like all aspects of divorce, taking one step at a time can help minimize your stress and uncertainty throughout the process.

11.1 What system does North Carolina use for dividing property?

Upon application by either party prior to divorce, North Carolina uses *equitable distribution* to divide marital assets and liabilities. Equitable distribution is a very complex area of law which contains a minefield of exceptions and a complex analysis. Generally speaking, equitable distribution uses a three-step process to determine the spouse's rights to assets and liabilities:

- Classify the assets as marital or separate.
- Value the assets as of the date of separation as well as when the assets are distributed.
- Equitably divide the assets.

11.2   What is the difference between *marital* and *separate* property?

To determine whether an asset is classified as marital or separate, you must look at how the property was earned or acquired. *Separate property* is property acquired before the marriage or from the labor of either spouse after the couple separated. If the property was acquired during the marriage, it is presumed to be *marital,* unless it was a gift or inheritance from one spouse's family or was bought with property acquired before marriage.

11.3   How is our property valued?

The property will be valued at the fair market value as of the date of separation and then again when it is to be distributed. The *fair market value* is how much the property would be sold for to a willing buyer. The values of some assets, such as bank accounts, are usually not disputed. The values of other assets, such as homes or personal property, are more likely to be disputed by a spouse.

If your case proceeds to trial, you may give your opinion of the value of property you own. You or your spouse may also have certain property appraised by an expert. In such cases it may be necessary to have the appraiser appear at trial to give testimony regarding the appraisal and the value of the asset.

If you own substantial assets for which the value is likely to be disputed, talk to your attorney early in your case about the benefits and costs of expert witnesses.

11.4   How is the marital property equitably divided?

North Carolina law provides for an equitable or fair, but not necessarily equal, division of the property and debts acquired during your marriage. North Carolina does presume that equal is equitable unless one of several factors would require an unequal division of property. The main factors to understand relate to your debts, the length of your marriage, your circumstances and those of your spouse, and the history of contributions to the marriage. The law does not include marital misconduct as one of the factors to be used in determining the equitable division of assets and debts of the marriage.

Regardless of how title is held, the court can use its discretion to make a division of the marital assets. In most cases this may mean an equal division, but in rare circumstances as little as 10 percent of the assets awarded to one party or 90 percent to the other has been considered "equitable."

11.5 What is meant by a *property inventory* and how detailed should mine be?

A *property inventory* is a listing of the property you own. It may also include a brief description of the property. Discuss with your attorney the level of inventory detail needed to benefit your case.

Factors to consider when creating your inventory may include:

- The extent to which you anticipate you and your spouse will disagree regarding the division of your property
- Whether you anticipate a dispute regarding the value of the property either you or your spouse retains
- Whether you will have continued access to the property if a later inventory is needed or whether your spouse will retain control of the property
- Whether you and your spouse are likely to disagree about which items are premarital, inherited, or gifts from someone other than your spouse

In addition to creating an inventory, your attorney may request that you prepare a list of the property that you and your spouse have already divided or a list of the items you want but your spouse has not agreed to give you.

If you do not have continued access to your property, talk to your attorney about asking your spouse or the court for access to the property to take photographs of the property to complete your inventory.

11.6 What does *date of distribution* mean?

Because the value of assets can go up or down while a divorce is pending, it can be necessary to determine and set up a second date for valuing the marital assets. This is referred to as the *date of distribution*. The passive increase or decrease of value from the date of separation to the date of distribution is called *divisible property*. The court will also divide the divisible property.

11.7 I've heard the old saying, "possession is nine-tenths of the law." Is that true during divorce proceedings?

It can be. Consulting with an attorney before the date of separation can reduce the risk that assets will be hidden, transferred, or destroyed by your spouse. This is especially important if your spouse has a history of destroying property, incurring substantial debt, or transferring money without your knowledge.

The possible actions you and your attorney can consider together include:

- Placing your family heirlooms or other valuables in a safe location
- Transferring some portion of financial accounts prior to separating
- Preparing an inventory of the personal property
- Taking photographs or a video of the property
- Obtaining copies of important financial records or statements

Plans to leave the marital home should also be discussed in detail with your attorney so that any actions taken early in your case are consistent with your ultimate goals. Speak candidly with your lawyer about your concerns so that a plan can be developed that provides a level of protection that is appropriate to your circumstances.

11.8 How are assets such as cars, boats, and furniture divided, and when does this happen?

The court values marital property as the fair market value on the date of separation. The value is not the purchase price of the goods, but rather what the sales price would be. In most cases, spouses are able to reach their own agreements about how to divide personal property, such as household furnishings and vehicles.

If you and your spouse disagree about how to divide certain items, it may be wise to consider which are truly valuable to you, financially or otherwise. Perhaps some of them can be easily replaced. Always look to see whether it is a good use of your attorney fees to argue over items of personal property. If a negotiated settlement cannot be reached, the issue of the division of your property will be made by the judge at trial.

11.9 How and when are liquid assets such as bank accounts and stocks divided?

Talk with your attorney early in your case about the benefits of a temporary restraining order or interim distribution of assets to reduce the risk that your spouse will transfer money out of financial accounts or transfer other assets.

In many cases couples will agree to divide bank accounts equally at the outset of the case. However, this may not be advisable in your case. Discuss with your attorney whether you should keep an accounting of how you spend money used from a bank account while your divorce is in progress.

Stocks are ordinarily a part of the final agreement for the division of property and debts. If you and your spouse cannot agree on how your investments should be divided, the judge will make the decision at trial.

11.10 How is it determined who gets the house?

The first issue regarding the family home is often a determination of who will retain possession of it while the divorce is pending. This determination is typically made by the spouses out of court. Later, it must be decided whether the house will be sold or whether it will be awarded to you or your spouse.

If you and your spouse are unable to reach an agreement regarding the house, the judge will decide who keeps it or whether it will be sold.

11.11 What is meant by *equity* in my home?

Regardless of who is awarded your house, the court will consider whether the spouse not receiving the house should be compensated for the equity in the house. By *equity* we mean the difference between the value of the home and the amount owed in mortgages against the property.

For example, if the first mortgage is $50,000 and the second mortgage from a home equity loan is $10,000, the total debt owed against the house is $60,000. If your home is valued at $200,000, the equity in your home is $140,000 (the $200,000 value less the $60,000 in mortgages equals $140,000 in equity).

If one of the parties remains in the home, the issue of how to give the other party his or her share of the equity must be considered.

11.12 How will the equity in our house be divided?

If your home is sold, the equity in the home will most likely be divided at the time of the sale, after the costs of the sale have been paid.

If either you or your spouse is awarded the house, there are a number of options for the other party being compensated for his or her share of the equity in the marital home. These could include:

- The spouse who does not receive the house receives other assets (for example, retirement funds or a stock account) to compensate for the value of the equity.
- The person who remains in the home agrees to refinance the home at some future date and to pay the other party his or her share of the equity.
- The parties agree for the property to be sold at a future date, or upon the happening of a certain event such as the youngest child completing high school or the remarriage of the party retaining the home. The parties then split the sales proceeds.

As the residence is often among the most valuable assets considered in a divorce, it is important that you and your attorney discuss the details of its disposition. These include:

- Appraisal of the property
- Refinancing to remove a party from liability for the mortgage
- The dates on which certain actions should be taken, such as listing the home for sale
- The real estate agent
- Costs of preparing the home for sale
- Making mortgage payments

If you and your spouse do not agree regarding which of you will remain in the home, the court will decide who keeps it or may order the sale of the property.

11.13 Should I sell the house during the divorce proceedings?

Selling your home is a big decision. To help you decide what is right for you, ask yourself these questions:

- How will selling the home impact my children?
- How much support do I anticipate receiving?
- Can I afford to stay in the house after the divorce?
- After the divorce, will I be willing to give the house and yard the time, money, and physical energy required for its maintenance?
- Will my spouse agree to the sale of the house?
- Is it necessary for me to sell the house to pay a share of the equity to my spouse, or are there other options?
- Would my life be easier if I were in a smaller or simpler home?
- Would I prefer to move closer to friends and family for support?
- What is the state of the housing market in my community?
- What are the benefits of remaining in this home?
- Can I retain the existing mortgage or will I have to refinance?

- Will I have a higher or lower interest rate if I sell the house?
- Can I see myself living in a different home?
- Will I have the means to acquire another home?
- If I don't retain the home and my spouse asks for it, what affect will this have on my custody case?
- What will the real estate commission be?
- How much will it cost to prepare the house for sale?

Selling a home is more than just a legal or financial decision. Consider what is important to you in creating your life after divorce when deciding whether to sell your home.

11.14 My mortgage broker told me that I have to title the house I owned before we got married as *husband and wife property* if I want to refinance. Will that cause me any problems?

It depends. Typically, title does not matter when determining whether an asset is considered marital or separate. However, North Carolina law considers transferring your separate real property into "tenants by the entirety" (titled as *husband's* and *wive's* names) as a gift to the marriage. This can be prevented if you have an attorney draft a special document indicating that the transfer is not intended to be a gift to the marriage.

11.15 Who keeps all the household goods until the decree is signed?

Either party can consider asking for an interim distribution of marital property at any time after the date of separation, however the court will ordinarily not decide who keeps the household goods on a temporary basis. Most couples attempt to resolve these issues on their own rather than incur legal fees to dispute household goods on a temporary basis.

11.16 What happens to our individual checking and savings accounts during and after the divorce?

The titled owner(s) will have the ability to access the accounts. Regardless of whose name is on the account, bank accounts may be considered marital assets and may be divided by the court. Therefore, the use and/or waste of assets will be accounted for in the separation agreement or court order.

Discuss with your attorney the benefits of a temporary restraining order or an interim distribution to protect bank accounts. Also ask your attorney how to use these accounts while the case is pending, and for the date on which financial accounts should be valued.

11.17 Do each one of our financial accounts have to be divided in half if we agree to an equal division of our assets?

No. Rather than incurring the administrative challenges and expense of dividing each asset in half, you and your spouse can decide that one of you will take certain assets equal to the value of assets taken by the spouse. If necessary, one of you can agree to make a cash payment to the other to make an equitable division.

11.18 Who gets the interest from such things as certificates of deposit, or dividends from stock holdings during the divorce proceedings?

Whether you or your spouse receives interest from these assets is decided as a part of the overall division of your property and debts.

11.19 Will debts be considered when determining the division of the property?

Yes. The court will consider the marital debts when dividing the property. For example, if you are awarded a car valued at $12,000, but you owe a $10,000 debt on the same vehicle, the court will take that debt into consideration in the overall division of the assets. Similarly, if one spouse agrees to pay substantial marital credit card debt, this obligation may also be considered in the final determination of the division of property and debts.

If your spouse incurred debts that you believe should be his or her sole responsibility, tell your attorney. Debts incurred that are not for the benefit of the marriage are not marital and are treated separately from other debts incurred during the marriage. For example, if your spouse spent large sums of money on gambling or illegal drugs without your knowledge, you may be able to argue that those debts should be the sole responsibility of your spouse.

11.20 Are all of the assets, such as property, bank accounts, and inheritances, that I had prior to my marriage, still going to be mine after the divorce?

It depends. In many cases the court will allow a party to retain an asset brought into the marriage, but the following are questions the court will consider in making its determination:

- Can the premarital asset be clearly traced? For example, if you continue to own a vehicle that you brought into the marriage, it is likely that it will be awarded to you. However, if you brought a vehicle into the marriage, sold it during the marriage, and spent the proceeds, you will not get the value of your separate property.

- Did you keep the property separate and titled in your name, or did you commingle it with marital assets? Premarital assets you kept separate may be more likely to be awarded to you. The separate portion of commingled assets must be isolated with proper documentation, which can be difficult to do.

- Did the other spouse contribute to the increase in the value of the premarital asset, and can the value of that increase be proven? For example, suppose a woman had $100,000 prior to marriage. After the parties married they begin a family business with the $100,000 of separate seed money from the wife. After ten years of marriage the family business is worth millions due to the efforts of husband and wife. At the time of the divorce, the husband seeks a portion of the equity in the family business. The court might consider the value of the business at the time of the marriage, any contributions to the increase in equity made by the husband, and the evidence of the value of those contributions.

11.21 Can I keep gifts and inheritances I received during the marriage?

Similar rules apply to gifts and inheritances received during the marriage as apply to premarital assets, that is, assets you owned prior to the marriage.

Gifts that you and your spouse gave to one another may be treated as any other marital asset. For gifts received during the marriage, such as a gift from a parent, the court will need to determine whether the gift was made to one party or to both. Whether you will be entitled to keep assets you inherited, assuming they are still in existence, will depend upon the unique circumstances of your case. When dividing the marital estate, the court may consider the fact that one spouse is allowed to keep substantial nonmarital assets such as an inheritance.

The following factors increase the probability that you will be entitled to keep your inheritance:

- The inheritance has been kept separate from the marital assets, such as in a separate account.
- The inheritance is titled in your name only.
- The inheritance has not been commingled with marital assets.
- Your spouse has not contributed to the care, operation, or improvement of the inheritance.

It is less likely that you will be awarded your full inheritance if:

- It was commingled with marital assets.
- Its origin cannot be traced.
- Your spouse has contributed to the increase in the value of the inheritance.

If keeping your inheritance is important to you, talk to your attorney about the information needed to build your case.

11.22 My spouse says I'm not entitled to a share of his stock options because he gets to keep them only if he stays employed with his company. What are my rights?

Stock options are often a very valuable asset. They are also one of the most complex issues when dividing assets during a divorce for these, among other, reasons:

- Each company has its own rules about awarding and exercising stock options.
- Complete information is needed from the employer.
- There are different methods for calculating the value of stock options.
- The reasons the options were given can impact the valuation. For example, some are given for future performance.
- There are cost and tax considerations when options are exercised.

Rather than being awarded a portion of the stock options themselves, you are likely to receive a share of the proceeds when the stock options are exercised.

If either you or your spouse owns stock options, begin discussing this asset with your attorney early in your case to allow sufficient time to settle the issues or to be well prepared for trial.

11.23 What is a *prenuptial agreement* and how might it affect the property settlement phase of the divorce?

A *prenuptial agreement,* sometimes referred to as a *premarital agreement,* is a contract entered into between two people prior to their marriage. It can include provisions for how assets and debts will be divided in the event the marriage is terminated, as well as terms concerning estate rights and alimony.

Your property settlement is likely to be impacted by the terms of your prenuptial agreement if the agreement is upheld as valid by the court.

11.24 Can a prenuptial agreement be contested during the divorce?

Yes. The court may consider many factors in determining whether to uphold your prenuptial agreement. Among them are:

- Whether your agreement was entered into voluntarily
- Whether your agreement was fair and reasonable at the time it was signed
- Whether you and your spouse each gave a complete disclosure of your assets and debts

- Whether you and your spouse each had your own lawyer
- Whether you and your spouse each had enough time to consider the agreement
- Whether the premarital agreement has provisions that are against public policy
- Whether the agreement terms are unambiguous

If you have a prenuptial agreement, take a copy of it to the initial consultation with your attorney. Be sure to provide your lawyer with a detailed history of the facts and circumstances surrounding reaching and signing the agreement.

11.25 My husband and I have owned and run our own business together for many years. Can I be forced out of it?

Deciding what should happen with a family business when divorce occurs can be a challenge. Because of the risk for future conflict between you and your spouse, the value of the business is likely to be substantially decreased if you both remain owners.

In discussing your options with your lawyer, consider the following questions:

- If one spouse retains ownership of the business, are there enough other assets for the other spouse to receive a fair share of the total marital assets?
- Which spouse has the skills and experience to continue running the business?
- What would you do if you weren't working in the business?
- What is the value of the business?
- What is the market for the business if it were to be sold?
- Could you remain an employee of the business for some period of time even if you were not an owner?

You and your spouse know your business best. With the help of your lawyers, you may be able to create a settlement that can satisfy you both. If not, the judge will make the decision for you at trial.

11.26 What factors determine whether I can get at least half of my spouse's business?

Many factors determine whether you will get a share of your spouse's business and in what form you might receive it. Among the factors the court will look at are:

- Whether your spouse owned the business prior to your marriage
- Your role, if any, in operating the business or increasing its value
- The overall division of the property and debts

If you or your husband own a business, it is important that you work with your attorney early in your case to develop a strategy for valuing the business and making your case for how it should be treated in the division of property and debts.

11.27 What is a *property settlement agreement*?

A *property settlement agreement* is a written document that includes all of the financial agreements you and your spouse have reached in your divorce. This may include the division of property, debts, child support, alimony, insurance, and attorney fees. The property settlement may be a separate document, or it may be incorporated into a court order.

11.28 I suspect my spouse is hiding assets, but I can't prove it. How can I protect myself if I discover later that I was right?

Ask your lawyer to include language in your settlement documents to address your concern. Insist that it include an acknowledgment by your spouse that the agreement was based upon a full and complete disclosure of your spouse's financial condition. Discuss with your lawyer a provision that allows for setting aside the agreement if it is later discovered that assets were hidden. You also can request that 60 percent or more of any hidden asset that is later discovered should be distributed to you upon discovery.

11.29 What happens after my spouse and I approve the *separation and property settlement agreement?* Do we still have to go to court?

Not necessarily. After you and your spouse sign your names to approve the *separation and property settlement agreement,* the financial issues resolved in that contract are finished and do not need court approval. If you resolve some or all of your claims with a consent order decree, it must still be approved by a judge, but it is typically done by the judge in chambers.

Some issues cannot be resolved by an out-of-court settlement document alone and may require a court order such as: a qualified domestic relations order to divide retirement accounts as well as your divorce decree.

11.30 If my spouse and I can't decide who gets what, who decides? Can the judge's decision be contested?

If you and your spouse cannot agree on the division of your property, the judge will make the determination after considering the evidence at your trial. If either party is dissatisfied with the decision reached by the judge, an appeal to a higher court is possible.

11.31 What happens to the property distribution if one of us dies before the divorce proceedings are completed?

If your spouse dies prior to your divorce decree being entered, you will be considered married and treated as a surviving spouse under the law. You still must either settle with your spouse's estate (heirs) or sue the estate to divide the marital property.

11.32 Will I get to keep my engagement ring?

North Carolina law is unclear on this issue. Typically, if your engagement ring was given to you prior to your marriage, it will likely be treated as your premarital property that you can keep.

11.33 I worked diligently for years to support my family while my spouse completed an advanced degree. Do I have a right to any of my spouse's future earnings?

No, not through the equitable distribution of your property. Your contributions during the marriage, however, are factors that will be considered in whether to provide you with an unequal division of the property and debts, as well as any award of alimony. Be sure to give your attorney a complete history of your contributions to the marriage and ask about their impact on the outcome of your case.

11.34 How is pet custody determined?

Pet custody is determined on a case-by-case basis. North Carolina law treats a pet as if it were personal property but pet owners know that a pet is more than just an item of furniture to be valued and distributed. The best interest of the dog is not the determinative factor, but judges typically take a reasoned approach as to who gets the family pets. The court may consider factors such as:

- Who held title to the pet?
- When was it purchased or acquired?
- What is the value of the pet now?
- Who provided care for the pet?
- Who will best be able to meet the pet's needs?
- Where is the child primarily residing?

If it is important to you to be awarded one of your family pets, discuss the matter with your attorney. It may be possible to reach a pet care agreement with your spouse that will allow you to share possession of and responsibility for your pets.

11.35 I'm Jewish and want my husband to cooperate with obtaining a *get cooperation clause,* which is a divorce document under our religion. Can I get a court order for this?

Talk to your lawyer about obtaining a *get cooperation clause* in your settlement documents including a provision regarding who should pay for it. At this time, the law regarding this issue has not been established in North Carolina.

11.36 Who will get the frozen embryo of my egg and my spouse's sperm that we have stored at the health clinic?

The law on this issue is not yet established in North Carolina. The terms of your contract with the clinic may impact the rights you and your spouse may have to the embryo, so provide a copy of it to your attorney for review. This area of law is changing rapidly, and legislation to resolve these kinds of issues were introduced recently. You should speak with an attorney about these issues. If permissible under your contract, you and your spouse may want to consider donating the embryo to another couple.

11.37 What does *community property* mean?

Community property is a term used in several states that have a community property system for dividing assets in a divorce. North Carolina is not a community-property state and community property laws do not apply.

11.38 How will our property in another state be divided?

For the purposes of dividing your assets, out-of-state property is treated the same as property in North Carolina. Although a North Carolina court cannot order a change in the title to property located in another state, a judge can order your spouse either to turn the property over to you or to sign a deed or other document to transfer title to you.

12

Benefits: Insurance, Retirement, and Pensions

During your marriage, you might have taken certain employment benefits for granted. You might not have given much thought each month to having insurance through your spouse's work. When you find yourself in a divorce, suddenly these benefits come to the forefront of your mind.

You might also, even unconsciously, have seen your own employment retirement benefits as belonging to you and not your spouse, referring to "My 401(k)" or "My pension." After all, you are the one who went to work every day to earn it, right?

When you divorce, some benefits arising from your spouse's employment will end, some may continue for a period of time, and others may be divided between you. Retirement funds, in particular, are often one of the most valuable marital assets to be divided in a divorce.

Whether the benefits are from your employer or your spouse's, with your attorney's help you will develop a better understanding of which benefits the law considers to be "yours," "mine," and "ours," for continuing or dividing.

12.1 Will my children continue to have health coverage through my spouse's work even though we're divorcing?

If either you or your spouse currently provides health insurance for your children, it is very likely that the court will order the insurance to remain in place for so long as it remains available and support is being paid for your child. The cost of

159

insurance for the children will be taken into consideration in determining the amount of child support to be paid.

12.2 Will I continue to have health insurance through my spouse's work after the divorce?

Yes, if you want to pay high premiums. Your coverage under your spouse's health insurance will end when you are divorced. You may be able to continue on your spouse's plan through a federal law known as *COBRA* (for companies with twenty or more employees) or through a North Carolina law nicknamed "mini-COBRA" (for companies with fewer than twenty employees).

Though you can continue your coverage through COBRA (for thirty-six months) or through mini-COBRA (for eighteen months), it may be a better idea to look elsewhere for less expensive insurance. If you are employed, after your divorce, your employer may provide health insurance enrollment in its plan even if you did not previously enroll. The *Patient Protection and Affordable Care Act (PPACA),* commonly referred to as "Obamacare," or the *Affordable Care Act (ACA),* may allow you to find less expensive health insurance than COBRA or mini-COBRA. The ACA allows you sixty days after you lose coverage because of divorce to apply for coverage under the ACA even if you are not in the annual open-enrollment period.

Begin early to investigate your options for your future health insurance. The cost of your health care is an important factor when pursuing spousal support and planning your post-divorce budget.

12.3 What is a *QMSO*?

A *qualified medical support order (QMSO)* is a court order requiring an employer's health insurers to enroll (or continue coverage for) a minor child under his or her parent's health insurance plan. A QMSO may also enable a parent to obtain other information about the plan without having to go through the parent who has the coverage. Rather than allowing only the parent with the insurance to be reimbursed for a claim, under a QMSO a health insurance plan is required to reimburse directly whoever actually paid the child's medical expense.

12.4 How many years must I have been married before I'm eligible to receive a part of my spouse's retirement fund or pension?

Even if your marriage is not of long duration, you may be entitled to a portion of your spouse's retirement fund or pension accumulated during the marriage. For example, if you were married for three years and your spouse contributed $10,000 to a 401(k) plan during the marriage, it is possible that the court would award you half of the value of the contribution when dividing your property and debts.

12.5 I contributed to my pension plan for ten years before I got married. Will my spouse get half of my entire pension?

Probably not. It is more likely the court will award your spouse only a portion of your retirement that was acquired during the marriage. For instance, if your pension plan vests after twenty years and you worked a total of twenty years (contributing to the pension for ten years during the marriage), then half of the pension would be considered marital property. In most circumstances, your spouse could receive no more than 50 percent of the marital property portion of the pension. If there are insufficient other marital assets for equitable distribution, if there is a business that is difficult to divide, or if the parties agree, then the court could award greater than 50 percent of the pension to your spouse.

If either you or your spouse made premarital contributions to a pension or retirement plan, be sure to let your attorney know. This information is essential to determine which portion of the retirement plan should be treated as premarital and thus unlikely to be shared.

12.6 I plan to keep my same job after my divorce. Will my former spouse get half of the money I contribute to my retirement plan after my divorce?

No. Your former spouse should be entitled to a portion of your retirement accumulated only during the marriage and prior to separation. Talk with your attorney so that the language of the court order ensures protection of your post-separation retirement contributions.

12.7 Am I still entitled to a share of my spouse's retirement even though I never contributed to one during our twenty-five-year marriage?

Probably. Retirements are often the most valuable asset accumulated during a marriage. Consequently, your judge will consider the retirement along with all of the other marital assets and debts when determining a fair division.

12.8 My lawyer says I'm entitled to a share of my spouse's retirement. How can I find out how much I get and when I'm eligible to receive it?

More than one factor will determine your rights to collect from your spouse's retirement. One factor will be the terms of the court order dividing the retirement. The court order will tell you whether you are entitled to a set dollar amount, a percentage, or a fraction to be determined based upon the length of your marriage and how long your spouse continues working.

Another factor will be the terms of the retirement plan itself. Some provide for lump sum withdrawals; others issue payments in monthly installments. Review the terms of your court order and contact the plan administrator to obtain the clearest understanding of your rights and benefits.

12.9 If I am eligible to receive my spouse's retirement benefits, do I have to be sixty-five years old to collect them?

It depends upon the terms of your spouse's retirement plan. In some cases, it is possible to begin receiving your share at the earliest date your spouse is eligible to receive them, regardless of whether he or she elects to do so. Check the terms of your spouse's plan to learn your options.

12.10 What happens if my former spouse is old enough to receive benefits but I'm not?

Ordinarily you will be eligible to begin receiving your share of the benefits when your former spouse begins receiving his or her benefits. Depending upon the plan, you may be eligible to receive them sooner.

12.11 Am I entitled to cost-of-living increases on my share of my spouse's retirement?

It depends. If your spouse has a retirement plan that includes a provision for a *cost-of-living allowance (COLA),* talk to your lawyer about whether this can be included in the court order dividing the retirement.

12.12 What circumstances might prevent me from getting part of my spouse's retirement benefits?

Some government pension plans are not subject to division. In addition, there are a few plans that are considered "non-qualified" and not subject to the same rules that allow direct assignment of retirement benefits. If you or your spouse are employed by a government agency or has a non-qualified plan, talk with your lawyer about how this may affect the property settlement in your case.

12.13 Does the death of my spouse affect the payout of retirement benefits to me or to our children?

It depends upon both the nature of your spouse's retirement plan and the terms of the court order dividing the retirement. If you want to be eligible for survivorship benefits from your spouse's pension, discuss the issue with your attorney before your case is settled or goes to trial. He or she can advise you.

Some plans allow only a surviving spouse or former spouse to be a beneficiary. Others may allow for the naming of an alternate beneficiary, such as your children.

12.14 How can I be sure I'll get my share of my former spouse's retirement when I am entitled to it years from now?

Rather than relying upon your former spouse to pay you a share of a future retirement, your best protection is a court order that provides for the retirement or pension plan administrator to pay the money directly to you. This type of court order is often referred to as a *qualified domestic relations order (QDRO)* or, in the case of federal retirement plans, a *court order acceptable for processing (COAP).* Such orders help ensure that a nonemployee spouse receives his or her share directly from the employee spouse's plan.

Obtaining a QDRO or COAP is a critical step in the divorce process. They can be complex documents, and a number of steps are required to reduce future concerns about enforcement and fully protect your rights. These court orders must comply with numerous technical rules and be approved by the plan administrator, which is often located outside North Carolina. Whenever possible, court orders dividing retirement plans should be entered at the same time as the decree of dissolution.

For some government or non-qualifying plans (plans not subject to QDRO), you must find ways (other than a QDRO) to receive the value you are entitled to. When dividing up other assets, a settlement or judgment can take into account the retirement that cannot be split. Your spouse may agree or be ordered to transfer a portion of the funds once he or she actually receives them from the plan, but there can be complicated tax issues with this method.

12.15 If my former spouse passes on before I do, can I still collect his or her Social Security benefits?

It depends. If you were married to your spouse for ten or more years and you have not remarried, you may be eligible for benefits. Contact your local Social Security Administration office or visit the SSA website at www.ssa.gov.

12.16 Because we share children, should I consider my spouse as a beneficiary on my life insurance?

You can consider your spouse as a beneficiary if you trust that the money will be used for your children rather than for your spouse. A better alternative would be to leave the money to the children in trust until they are old enough to spend it wisely. Talk to your attorney about your options.

12.17 My spouse is in the military. What are my rights to benefits after the divorce?

As the former spouse of a military member, the types of benefits to which you may be entitled are typically determined by the number of years you were married, the number of years your spouse was in the military while you were married, and whether you have remarried. Be sure you obtain accurate information about these dates.

Among the benefits for which you may be eligible include:

- A portion of your spouse's military retirement pay
- A survivor benefit in the event of your spouse's death
- Health care or participation in a temporary, transitional health care program
- Use of certain military facilities, such as the commissary

While your divorce is pending, educate yourself about your right to future military benefits so that you can plan for your future with clarity. If your divorce is still pending, contact your base's legal office, or, for more information, visit the website for the branch of the military of which your spouse was a member.

13

Division of Debts

Throughout a marriage, most couples will have disagreements about money from time to time. You might think extra money should be spent on a family vacation, and your spouse might insist it should be saved for your retirement. You might think it's time you finally get a new car, and your spouse thinks you would be fine driving the ten-year-old van for two more years.

If you and your spouse had different philosophies about saving and spending during your marriage, chances are you will have some differing opinions when dividing your debts in divorce. What you both can count on is that North Carolina law provides that, to reach a fair outcome, the payment of debts must also be taken into consideration when dividing the assets from your marriage.

There are steps you can take to ensure the best outcome possible when it comes to dividing your marital debt. These include providing accurate and complete debt information to your lawyer and asking your lawyer to include provisions to protect you in the future in your settlement documents if your spouse refuses to pay his or her share.

Regardless of how the debts from your marriage are divided, know that you will gradually build your independent financial success when making a fresh start after your divorce is final.

13.1 Who is responsible for paying credit card bills and making house payments during the divorce proceedings?

Work with your attorney and your spouse to reach a temporary agreement on who will pay the debts. Discuss the importance of making at least minimum payments on time to avoid substantial finance charges and late fees. These issues may be resolved by the court in a temporary spousal support award or through the use of an interim distribution of marital property and/or debts.

Usually, the spouse who remains in the home will be responsible for the mortgage payments, taxes, utilities, and most other ordinary expenses related to the house. Sometimes the mortgage will be apportioned between the parties or addressed in the spousal support order. If you are concerned that you cannot afford to stay in the marital home on a temporary basis, talk with your attorney about your options prior to your temporary hearing.

13.2 What, if anything, should I be doing with the credit card companies as we go through the divorce?

If possible, it is best to obtain some separate credit prior to the divorce. This will help you establish credit in your own name and help you with necessary purchases following a separation.

Begin by obtaining a copy of your credit report from at least two of the three nationwide consumer reporting companies: Experian, Equifax, or TransUnion. The *Fair Credit Reporting Act* entitles you a free copy of your credit report from each of these three companies every twelve months.

Your spouse may have incurred debt using your name. This information is important to relay to your attorney. If you and your spouse have joint credit card accounts, contact any credit card company to close the account. Do the same if your spouse is an authorized user on any of your accounts.

If you want to maintain credit with a company, ask to have a new account in your own name. Be sure to let your spouse know if you close an account he or she has been using.

13.3　How is credit card debt divided?

Credit card debt will be divided as a part of the overall division of the marital property and debts. Just as in the division of property, the court considers what is equitable, or fair, in your case.

If your spouse has exclusively used a credit card for purposes that did not benefit the family, such as gambling, or for an affair, talk with your attorney. For a debt to be marital your spouse will have to show he used the credit card for marital purposes.

13.4　Am I responsible for repayment of my spouse's student loans?

It depends. If your spouse incurred student loans prior to the marriage, these loans are your spouse's separate debt. If the debt was incurred during the marriage, however, the court will need to determine if the student loan was for a marital purpose. If the loan was for a marital purpose, then it will be considered marital debt. For example, if the student loan debt was incurred to help your spouse obtain a higher paying job and your spouse did increase his or her salary during the marriage as a result, then the court may consider the student loans a marital debt.

If you were a joint borrower on your spouse's student loan and your spouse fails to pay the loan, the lender may attempt to collect from you even if your spouse has been ordered to pay the debt.

If either you or your spouse has student loan debt, be sure to give your attorney the complete history regarding the debt and ask about the most likely outcome under the facts of your case.

13.5　During the divorce proceedings, am I still responsible for debt my spouse continues to accrue?

It depends. In most cases the court will order each of the parties to be responsible for his or her own post-separation debts.

13.6 During the marriage my spouse applied for and received several credit cards without my knowledge. Am I responsible for them?

It depends. If the debts were not for a marital purpose, then they may be your spouse's separate debt. The court will consider the overall fairness of the property and debt division when deciding who should pay this debt. If your spouse bought items with the cards and intends to keep those items, it is likely that he or she will be ordered to pay the debt incurred for the purchases.

The credit card companies are unlikely to be able to pursue collection from you for the debt unless your spouse used them for necessities of life, such as food, necessary clothing, or housing.

13.7 During our marriage, we paid off thousands of dollars of debt incurred by my spouse before we were married. Will the court take this into consideration when dividing our property and debt?

Just as premarital assets can have an impact on the overall division of property and debts, so can premarital debt. Depending upon the length of the marriage, the evidence of the debt, and the amount paid, it may be a factor for the judge to consider. The court might order that you receive an unequal division of the net marital property. Be sure to let your attorney know if either you or your spouse brought substantial debt into the marriage.

13.8 Regarding debts, what is a *hold-harmless clause,* and why should it be in our settlement documents?

A *hold-harmless clause* is intended to protect you in the event that your spouse fails to follow a court order to pay a debt after the divorce is granted. The language typically provides that your spouse shall "indemnify and hold (you) harmless from liability" on the debt.

If you and your spouse have a joint debt and your spouse fails to pay, the creditor may nevertheless attempt to collect from you. This is because the court is without power to change the creditor's rights, and can make orders affecting only you and your spouse.

In the event your spouse fails to pay a court-ordered debt and the creditor attempts collection from you, the hold-harmless provision in your settlement documents can be used in an effort to insist that your former spouse make payment on the debt.

13.9 Why do my former spouse's doctors say they have a legal right to collect from me when my former spouse was ordered to pay her own medical bills?

Under North Carolina law, you may be held liable for the "necessaries" of your spouse, such as health care costs and debts unless you notify the creditor of your separation prior to the charges being made or you are already divorced. Your settlement documents do not take away the legal rights of creditors to collect debts. Contact your attorney about how to minimize your risks related to the "doctrine of necessaries."

13.10 My spouse and I have agreed that I will keep our home; why must I refinance the mortgage?

There may be a number of reasons why your spouse is asking you to refinance the mortgage. First, the mortgage company cannot be forced to take your spouse's name off of the mortgage note. This means that if you did not make the house payments, the lender could pursue collection against your spouse.

Second, your spouse may not want to wait to receive a share of the home equity. It may be possible for you to borrow additional money at the time of refinancing to pay your spouse his or her share of the equity in the home.

Third, the mortgage on your family home may prevent your spouse from buying a home in the future. Because there remains a risk that your spouse could be pursued for the debt to the mortgage company, it is unlikely that a second lender will want to take the risk of extending further credit to your spouse.

13.11 Can I file for bankruptcy while my divorce is pending?

Consult with your attorney if you are considering filing for bankruptcy while your divorce is pending. It will be important for you to ask yourself a number of questions, such as:

- Should I file for bankruptcy on my own or with my spouse?
- How will my filing for bankruptcy affect my ability to purchase a home in the future?
- Which debts can be discharged in bankruptcy, and which cannot?
- How will a bankruptcy affect the division of property and debts in the divorce?
- How might a delay in the divorce proceedings due to a bankruptcy impact my case?
- Which form of bankruptcy is best for my situation?

If you use a different attorney for your bankruptcy than you have for your divorce, be sure that each attorney is kept fully informed about the developments in the other case.

13.12   What happens if my spouse files for bankruptcy during our divorce?

Contact your attorney right away. The filing of a bankruptcy while your divorce is pending can have a significant impact on your divorce. Your attorney can advise you whether certain debts are likely to be discharged in the bankruptcy, the delay a bankruptcy may cause to your divorce, and whether bankruptcy is an appropriate option for you. Also, the bankruptcy documents your spouse files will contain information you may otherwise have difficulties acquiring.

13.13   Can I file divorce while I am in bankruptcy?

Yes, however, you must receive the bankruptcy court's approval with the divorce. While in bankruptcy, your property is protected from debt collection by the "automatic stay." The stay can also prevent the divorce court from dividing property between you and your spouse until you obtain the bankruptcy court's permission to proceed with the divorce.

13.14   What should I do if my former spouse files for bankruptcy after our divorce?

Contact your attorney immediately. If you learn that your former spouse has filed for bankruptcy, you may have certain rights to object to the discharge of any debts your spouse was ordered to pay under your divorce decree. If you fail to take action, it is possible that you will be held responsible for debts your spouse was ordered to pay.

14

Taxes

Nobody likes a surprise letter from the Internal Revenue Service demanding more taxes. When your divorce is over, you want to be sure that you do not later discover you owe taxes you weren't expecting to pay.

A number of tax issues may arise in your divorce. Your attorney may not be able to answer all of your tax questions, so consulting your accountant or tax advisor for additional advice might be necessary.

Taxes are important considerations in both settlement negotiations and trial preparation. They should not be overlooked. Taxes can impact many of your decisions including those regarding alimony, division of property, and the receipt of benefits.

Be sure to ask the professionals helping you about the tax implications in your divorce so you do not get that letter in the mail that begins, "Dear Taxpayer:..."

14.1 Will either my spouse or I have to pay income tax when we transfer property or pay a property settlement to one another according to our divorce decree or settlement documents?

No. However, it is important that you see the future tax consequences of a subsequent withdrawal, sale, or transfer of certain assets you receive in your divorce. Make sure that your attorney takes tax consequences into consideration when looking at the division of your assets.

14.2   Is the amount of child support I pay tax deductible?
No.

14.3   Do I have to pay income tax on any child support I receive?
No. Your child support is tax-free regardless of when it is paid or when it is received.

14.4   Is the amount of alimony I pay tax deductible?
Yes, as long as it is truly alimony. The IRS considers a payment alimony if all of the following requirements are met:

- It is cash.
- It is made according to a divorce or separation instrument.
- It is not designated as not alimony.
- The spouses are not living in the same household when the payment is made.
- There is no requirement that the payment be made after the death of the recipient.
- The payment is not treated as child support.

Spousal support that is paid according to a court order and that meets the IRS requirements for alimony is deductible. This will include court-ordered alimony and may also include other forms of support provided to your former spouse (but not child support). IRS Publication 504, Divorced or Separated Individuals, (available at the IRS website at www.irs.gov) provides more detail on tax issues while you are going through a divorce.

14.5   Do I have to pay tax on the alimony I receive?
Yes, if it is truly alimony. You must pay income tax on the spousal support you receive. This will include court-ordered alimony and may also include other forms of spousal support, but not child support, paid by your spouse.

Income tax is a critical factor in determining a fair amount of alimony. Insist that your attorney bring this issue to the attention of your spouse's lawyer, or to the judge, if your case proceeds to trial, so that both the tax you pay and the deduction your spouse receives are taken into consideration.

Be sure to consult with your tax advisor about payment of tax on your spousal support. Making estimated tax payments throughout the year or withholding additional taxes from your wages can avoid a burdensome tax liability at the end of the year.

It is important to budget for payment of tax on your alimony. Taxes are also another item to consider when looking at your monthly living expenses for the purposes of seeking an alimony award.

14.6　During the divorce proceedings, is our tax filing status affected?

It can be. You are considered unmarried if your judgment of divorce or your separation agreement sanctioned by the court (by decree or judgment) is final by December 31 of the tax year.

If you are considered unmarried, your filing status is either "single" or, under certain circumstances, "head of household." If your judgment is not final as of December 31, your filing status is either "married filing a joint return" or "married filing a separate return," unless you live apart from your spouse and meet the exception for "head of household."

While your divorce is in progress, talk to both your tax advisor and your attorney about your filing status. It may be beneficial to figure your tax on both a joint return and a separate return to see which gives you the lower tax.

14.7　Should I file a joint income tax return with my spouse while our divorce is pending?

Consult your tax advisor to determine the risks and benefits of filing a joint return with your spouse. Compare this with the consequences of filing your tax return separately. Often the overall tax liability will be less with the filing of a joint return, but other factors are important to consider.

When deciding whether to file a joint return with your spouse, consider any concerns you have about the accuracy and truthfulness of the information on the tax return. If you have any doubts, consult both your attorney and your tax advisor before agreeing to sign a joint tax return with your spouse. Prior to filing a return with your spouse, try to reach an agreement about how any tax owed or refund expected will be shared, and ask your lawyer to assist you in getting this agreement in writing.

14.8 For tax purposes, is one time of year better to divorce than another?

It depends upon your tax situation. If you and your spouse agree that it would be beneficial to file joint tax returns for the year in which you are divorcing, you may not wish to have your divorce finalized before the end of the year.

Your marital status for filing income taxes is determined by your status on December 31.

14.9 What tax consequences should I consider regarding the sale of our home?

When your home is sold, whether during your divorce or after, the sale may be subject to a *capital gains tax*. If your home was your primary residence and you lived in the home for two of the preceding five years, you may be eligible to exclude up to $250,000 of the gain on the sale of your home. If both you and your spouse meet the ownership and residence tests, you may be eligible to exclude up to $500,000 of the gain.

If you anticipate the gain on the sale of your residence to be over $250,000, talk with your attorney early in the divorce process about a plan to minimize the tax liability. For more information, *see* IRS Publication 523, Selling Your Home, or visit the IRS website at www.irs.gov and talk with your tax advisor.

14.10 How might capital gains tax be a problem for me years after the divorce?

Future capital gains tax on the sale of property should be discussed with your attorney during the negotiation and trial preparation stages of your case. This is especially important if the sale of the property is imminent. Failure to do so may result in an unfair outcome.

For example, suppose you agree that your spouse will be awarded the proceeds from the sale of your home valued at $200,000, after the real estate commission, and you will take the stock portfolio also valued at $200,000.

After the divorce, you decide to sell the stock. It is still valued at $200,000, but you learn that its original price was $100,000 and that you must pay capital gains tax of 20 percent on the $100,000 gain. You pay tax of $20,000, leaving you with $180,000.

Meanwhile, your former spouse sells the marital home but pays no capital gains tax because he or she qualifies for the $250,000 exemption. He or she is left with the full $200,000.

Tax implications of your property division should always be discussed with your attorney, with support from your tax advisor as needed.

14.11 During and after the divorce, who gets to claim the children as dependents?

This issue should be addressed in settlement negotiations or at trial, if settlement is not reached. The judge has discretion to determine which parent will be entitled to claim the children as exemptions for income tax purposes. The *North Carolina Child Support Guidelines* assume the parent who receives child support claims the tax exemptions for the child and this is typically the case. Many judges order that the exemptions be shared or alternated. If one party has income so low or so high that he or she will not benefit from the dependency exemption, the court may award the exemption to the other parent.

14.12 I was ordered to sign IRS Form 8332 so my former spouse can claim our child as an exemption, because I have custody. Should I sign it once for all future years?

No. Child custody and child support can be modified in the future. If there is a future modification of custody or support, the parent that is entitled to claim your child as an exemption could change. The safest practice is to provide your former spouse a timely copy of Form 8332 signed by you for the appropriate tax year only. You can also provide your former spouse a timely copy of Form 8332 signed by you for a limited number of future years designated by you. If child custody or child support is modified in the future, you must be sure to provide your former spouse a timely copy of Form 8332 signed by you revoking your previous Form 8332.

14.13   Can my spouse and I split the child-care tax credit?

According to the *North Carolina Child Support Guidelines,* the value of the federal income tax credit for child care may be considered when determining the payor spouse's obligation to contribute to child-care expenses. Only the custodial parent is allowed to claim the credit. If you are a noncustodial parent and paying child care, talk to your lawyer about how to address this issue in your judgment or separation agreement.

14.14   Is the cost of getting a divorce, including my attorney fees, tax deductible under any circumstances?

Your legal fees for getting a divorce are not tax deductible. However, a portion of your attorney fees may be deductible if they are for:

- The collection of sums included in your gross income, such as alimony or interest income
- Advice regarding the determination of taxes or tax due

Attorney fees are "miscellaneous" deductions for individuals and consequently are limited to 2 percent of your adjusted gross income. More details can be found in IRS Publication 529, Miscellaneous Deductions, available on the IRS website at www.irs.gov.

You may also be able to deduct fees you pay to appraisers or accountants who help. Talk to your tax advisor about whether any portion of your attorney fees or other expenses from your divorce are deductible.

14.15   Do I have to complete a new Form W-4 for my employer because of my divorce?

Completing a new Form W-4, Employee's Withholding Certificate, will help you to claim the proper withholding allowances based upon your marital status and exemptions. Also, if you are receiving alimony, you may need to make quarterly estimated tax payments. Consult with your tax advisor to ensure you are making the most preferable tax planning decision.

14.16   What is *innocent spouse relief* and how can it help me?

Innocent spouse relief refers to a method of obtaining relief from the Internal Revenue Service for taxes owed as a result of a joint income tax return filed during your marriage.

Numerous factors affect your eligibility for innocent spouse tax relief, such as:

- You would suffer a financial hardship if you were required to pay the tax.
- You did not significantly benefit from the unpaid taxes.
- You suffered abuse during your marriage.
- You thought your spouse would pay the taxes on the original return.

Talk with your attorney or your tax advisor if you are concerned about liability for taxes arising from joint tax returns filed during the marriage. You may benefit from a referral to an attorney who specializes in tax law.

15

Going to Court

For many of us, our images of going to court are created by movie scenes and our favorite television shows. We picture the witness breaking down in tears after a grueling cross-examination. We see lawyers strutting around the courtroom, waving their arms as they plead their case to the jury.

Hollywood drama, however, is a far cry from reality. Going to court for your divorce can mean many things, ranging from sitting in a hallway while waiting for the lawyers and judges to conclude a conference, to being on the witness stand giving mundane answers to questions about your monthly living expenses.

Regardless of the nature of your court proceeding, going to court often evokes a sense of anxiety. Perhaps your divorce might be the first time in your life that you have even been in a courtroom. Be assured that these feelings of nervousness and uncertainty are normal.

Understanding what will occur in court and being well prepared for any court hearings will relieve much of your stress. Knowing the order of events, the role of the people in the courtroom, courtroom etiquette, and what is expected of you will make the entire experience easier.

Your lawyer will be with you at all times to support you any time you go to court. Remember, every court appearance moves you one step closer to completing your divorce so that you can move forward with your life.

15.1 What do I need to know about appearing in court and court dates in general?

Court dates are important. As soon as you receive a notice from your attorney about a court date in your case, confirm whether your attendance will be required and put it on your calendar. Ask whether it is necessary for you to meet with your attorney or take any other action to prepare for the hearing, such as providing additional information or documents.

Ask your attorney about the nature of the hearing, including whether the judge will be listening to testimony by witnesses, reading affidavits, or merely listening to the arguments of the lawyers. Find out how long the hearing is expected to last. It may be as short as a few minutes or as long as a day or more.

If you plan to attend the hearing, determine where and when to meet your attorney. Depending upon the type of hearing, your lawyer may want you to arrive in advance of the scheduled hearing time to prepare.

Make sure you know the location of the courthouse, where to park, and the floor and room number of the courtroom. Planning for such simple matters as change for a parking meter can eliminate unnecessary stress. If you want someone to go to court with you to provide you support, check with your attorney first.

15.2 When and how often will I need to go to court?

Whether and how often you will need to go to court depend upon a number of factors. Depending upon the complexity of your case, you may have only one hearing or numerous court hearings throughout the course of your divorce.

Some hearings, usually those on procedural matters, are attended only by the attorneys. These could include requests for the other side to provide information or for the setting of certain deadlines. These hearings are often brief and are sometimes held in the judge's chambers rather than in the courtroom. Other hearings, such as temporary hearings for custody or support, are typically attended by both parties and their attorneys.

If you and your spouse settle all of the issues in your case, a final hearing may be held, depending on the judge or county in which your case resides. Either you or your spouse, neither of you, or both of you, depending upon your situation, may be required to attend this brief hearing.

If your case proceeds to trial, your appearance will be required for the duration of the trial. In North Carolina, juries are extremely rare in divorce cases, as most matters related to divorce are heard before a judge only.

15.3   How much notice will I get about appearing in court?

The amount of notice you will get for any court hearing can vary from a few days to several weeks. Ask your attorney whether and when it will be necessary for you to appear in court on your case so that you can have ease in preparing and planning.

If you receive a notice of a hearing, contact your attorney immediately. He or she can tell you whether your appearance is required and what other steps are needed to prepare.

15.4   I am afraid to be alone in the same room with my spouse. When I go to court, is this going to happen if the lawyers go into the judge's office to discuss the case?

Talk to your lawyer. Prior to any court hearing, you and your spouse may be asked to wait while your attorneys meet with the judge to discuss preliminary matters.

A number of options are likely available to ensure that you feel safe. These might include having you or your spouse wait in different locations or having a friend or family member present.

Your lawyer wants to support you in feeling secure throughout all court proceedings. Just let him or her know your concerns.

15.5   Do I have to go to court every time there is a court hearing on any motion?

Not necessarily. Some matters will be decided by the judge after listening to the arguments of the lawyers. These hearings are sometimes held in the judge's office, referred to as "chambers," and you will not be required to attend.

15.6 My spouse's lawyer keeps asking for *continuances of court dates*. Is there anything I can do to stop this?

Continuances of court dates are not unusual in divorces. A court date might be postponed for many reasons, including a conflict on the calendar of one of the attorneys or the judge, the lack of availability of one of the parties or an important witness, or the need for more time to prepare.

Discuss with your attorney your desire to move your case forward without further delay, so that your attorney can vigorously resist repeated requests for continuances.

15.7 If I have to go to court, will I be put on the stand? Will there be a jury?

In North Carolina, divorce matters are almost universally heard before a judge only; juries rarely, if ever, are convened in divorce cases. Whether you will be put on the stand will depend upon the nature of the issues in dispute, the judge assigned to your case, and your attorney's strategy for your case.

15.8 My lawyer said I need to be in court for our temporary hearing next week. What's going to happen?

Temporary hearings are held to determine such matters as who remains in the house while your divorce is pending, temporary custody, and temporary support. The procedure for your temporary hearing can vary depending upon the county in which your case was filed, the judge to which the case is assigned, and whether temporary custody is disputed.

Temporary hearings may be held on the basis of written affidavits and the arguments of the lawyers. Although you should plan to attend your temporary hearing, it is possible that the hearing will be held in the judge's chambers with only the judge and attorneys present.

Even if you will not be testifying at your temporary hearing, your presence at the hearing is still important. Your attorney may need additional information from you during the hearing, and last-minute negotiations to resolve temporary issues are not uncommon.

In some counties, your hearing will be one of numerous other hearings. You may find yourself in a courtroom with many other lawyers and their clients, all having matters scheduled before the court that day.

If temporary custody is disputed, you and other witnesses might be required to take the witness stand to give testimony at your temporary hearing. If this is the case, meeting with your attorney in advance to fully prepare is very important.

Talk to your lawyer about the procedure you should expect for the temporary hearing in your case.

15.9 Do I have to go to court if all of the issues in my case are settled?

Usually not. In most counties, the attorneys and their clients can enter into consent orders to take care of any issues that need court approval. There are times that one of the parties may have to appear in court to obtain an uncontested final divorce decree, though most of the time this can be handled summarily with the attorneys.

15.10 Are there any rules about courtroom etiquette that I need to know?

Knowing a few tips about being in the courtroom will make your experience easier.

- Dress appropriately. Avoid overly casual dress, lots of jewelry, revealing clothing, and extreme hairstyles.
- Do not bring beverages into the courtroom. Most courts have rules that do not allow food and drink in courtrooms. If you need water, ask your lawyer.
- Dispose of chewing gum before giving testimony.
- Do not talk aloud in the courtroom unless you are on the witness stand or being questioned by the judge.
- Do not enter the judge's chambers.
- Stand up whenever the judge is entering or leaving the courtroom.
- Be sure to turn off your cell phone, pager, and electronic devices that make noise.

Although you may feel anxious initially, you will likely feel more relaxed about the courtroom setting once your hearing gets underway.

15.11 What is the role of the *bailiff*?

The *bailiff* is a deputy sheriff who enforces the court's orders and maintains security. The bailiff provides support for the judge and lawyers in the management of the courtroom.

15.12 Will there be a *court reporter*, and what will he or she do?

A *court reporter* is a professional trained to make an accurate record of the words spoken and documents offered into evidence during court proceedings. Some counties use audio or video recording devices rather than court reporters.

A written transcript of a court proceeding may be purchased from the court reporter. If your case is appealed, the transcript prepared by the court reporter will be used by the appeals court to review the facts of your case.

Some proceedings are held "off the record," which means that the court reporter is not making a record of what is being said. Ordinarily these are matters for which no appeal is expected to be taken.

15.13 Will I be able to talk to my attorney while we are in court?

During court proceedings it is important that your attorney give his or her full attention to anything being said by the judge, witnesses, or your spouse's lawyer. For this reason, your attorney will avoid talking with you when anyone else in the courtroom is speaking.

Plan to have pen and paper with you when you go to court. If your court proceeding is underway and your lawyer is listening to what is being said by others in the courtroom, write him or her a note with your questions or comments.

It is critical that your attorney hear each question asked by the other lawyer and all answers given by each witness. If not, opportunities for making objections to inappropriate evidence may be lost. You can support your attorney in doing an effective job for you by avoiding talking to him or her while a court hearing is in progress.

If your court hearing is lengthy, breaks will be taken. You can use this time to discuss with your attorney any questions or observations you have about the proceeding.

15.14 Besides meeting with my lawyer, is there anything else I should do to prepare for my upcoming trial?

Yes. Be sure to review your deposition and any information you provided in your discovery, such as answers to interrogatories. At trial, it is possible that you will be asked some of the same questions. If you think you might give different answers at trial, discuss this with your lawyer.

It is important that your attorney know in advance of trial whether any information you provided during the discovery process has changed.

15.15 I'm meeting with my lawyer to prepare for trial. How do I make the most of these meetings?

Meeting with your lawyer to prepare for your trial is important to achieving a good outcome. Come to the meeting prepared to discuss the following:

- The issues in your case
- Your desired outcome on each of the issues
- The questions you might be asked at trial by both lawyers
- The exhibits that will be offered into evidence during the trial
- The witnesses for your trial
- The status of negotiations

Your meeting with your lawyer will help you better understand what to expect at your trial and make the trial experience easier.

15.16 My lawyer says that the law firm is busy with *trial preparation*. What exactly is my lawyer doing to prepare for my trial?

Countless tasks are necessary to prepare your case for trial. These are just some of them:

- Developing arguments to be made on each of the contested issues
- Researching and reviewing the relevant law in your case

- Reviewing the facts of your case to determine which witnesses are best suited to testify about them
- Reviewing, selecting, and preparing exhibits
- Preparing questions for all witnesses
- Preparing an opening statement
- Reviewing rules on evidence to prepare for any objections to be made or opposed at trial
- Determining the order of witnesses and all exhibits
- Preparing your file for the day of court, including preparing a trial notebook with essential information

Your lawyer is committed to a good outcome for you in your divorce. He or she will be engaged in many important actions to fully prepare your case for trial.

15.17 My divorce is scheduled for trial. Does this mean there is no hope for a settlement?

Many cases are settled after a trial date is set. The setting of a trial date may cause you and your spouse to think about the risks and costs of going to trial. This can help you and your spouse focus on what is most important to you and lead you toward a negotiated settlement. Because the costs of preparing for and proceeding to trial are substantial, it is best to engage in settlement negotiations well in advance of your trial date.

15.18 Can I prevent my spouse from being in the courtroom?

Probably not. Because your spouse has a legal interest in the outcome of your divorce, he or she has a right to be present. North Carolina courtrooms are open to the public, and it is not uncommon even for persons uninvolved in your divorce to pass through the courtroom at various times simply because they have other business with the court.

15.19 Can I take a friend or family member with me to court?

Yes. Let your attorney know in advance whether you intend to bring anyone to court with you. Some people important to you may be very emotional about your divorce or your spouse. Be sure to invite someone who is better able to focus attention on supporting you rather than on his or her own feelings.

15.20 Can my friends and family be present in the courtroom during my entire trial?

It depends upon whether they will be witnesses in your case. In some cases, where witnesses other than the husband and wife are testifying, the attorneys request that the court "sequester" the witnesses. The judge could then order all witnesses, except you and your spouse, to leave the courtroom until after they have testified.

Once a witness has completed his or her testimony, he or she will ordinarily be allowed to remain in the courtroom for the remainder of the trial.

15.21 I want to do a good job testifying as a witness in my divorce trial. What are some tips?

Keep the following in mind to be a good witness on your own behalf:

- Tell the truth. While this may not always be comfortable, it is critical if you want your testimony to be believed by the judge.

- Listen carefully to the complete question before thinking of your answer. Wait to consider your answer until after the full question is asked.

- Slow down. It is easy to speed up your speech when you are anxious. Taking your time with your answers ensures that the judge hears you and that the court reporter can accurately record your testimony.

- If you don't understand a question or don't know the answer, be sure to say so.

- If the question calls for a "yes" or "no" answer, simply say yes or no, then wait for the attorney to ask you the next question. If there is more you want to explain, remember that you have already told your attorney all of the important facts and he or she will make sure you are allowed to give any testimony significant in your case.

- Do not argue with the judge or the lawyers.

- Take your time. You may be asked some questions that call for a thoughtful response. If you need a moment to reflect on an answer before you give it, allow yourself that time.

- Stop speaking if an objection is made by one of the lawyers. Wait until the judge has decided whether to allow you to answer.

15.22 Should I be worried about being cross-examined by my spouse's lawyer at trial?

If your case goes to trial, prepare to be asked some questions by your spouse's lawyer. Many of these questions will call for a simple "yes" or "no." It is a good idea to practice by having your own attorney conduct a mock cross-examination of you prior to trial.

If you are worried about particular questions, discuss your concerns with your attorney. He or she can support you in giving a truthful response. Focus on preparing well for being asked questions by your spouse's lawyer. Try not take the questions personally; remember that the lawyer is fulfilling a duty to advocate for your spouse's interests. Remember that you are just doing your best to tell the truth about the facts.

15.23 What happens on the day of trial?

Although no two trials are alike, the following steps will occur in most divorce trials:

- Attorneys may meet with the judge to discuss procedural issues, such as how many witnesses will be called, how long the case will take to present, and when breaks might be taken.
- Attorneys give opening statements.
- Plaintiff's attorney calls plaintiff's witnesses to testify. Defendant's attorney may cross-examine each of them.
- Defendant's attorney calls defendant's witnesses to testify. Plaintiff's attorney may cross-examine each of them.
- Plaintiff's lawyer calls any rebuttal witnesses, that is, witnesses whose testimony contradicts the testimony of the defendant's witnesses.
- Closing arguments are made first by plaintiff's attorney and then by defendant's attorney.

15.24 Will the judge decide my case the day I go to court?

Possibly. Often, however, there is so much information from the trial for the judge to consider that it is not possible for the judge to give an immediate ruling.

The judge may want to review documents, review the law, perform calculations, review his or her notes, and give thoughtful consideration to the issues to be decided. For this reason, it may be days, weeks, or in some cases, even longer before a ruling is made.

When a judge does not make a ruling immediately upon the conclusion of a trial, it is said that the case has been "taken under advisement."

16

The Appeals Process

Y ou may find that despite your best efforts to settle your case, your divorce went to trial and the judge made major decisions that will have a serious impact on your future. You may be either gravely disappointed or even shocked by the judge's ruling.

The judge might have seen your case differently than you and your attorney did. Perhaps the judge made mistakes. Or it may be that North Carolina law simply does not allow for the outcome you were hoping for.

Whatever the reasons for the court's rulings, you may feel that the judge's decisions are not ones that you can live with. If this is the case, talk to your lawyer immediately about your right to appeal. Together you can decide whether an appeal is in your best interest, or whether it is better to accept the court's ruling and invest your energy in moving forward with your future without an appeal.

16.1 How much time after my divorce do I have to file an appeal?

You must file an appeal within thirty days of the final order you wish to appeal. Because your attorney may also recommend filing certain motions following your trial, discuss your appeal rights with your lawyer as soon as you have received the judge's ruling.

A timely discussion with your attorney about your right to appeal is essential so important deadlines are not missed.

16.2   Can I appeal a temporary order?

No. Under North Carolina law, only final orders may be appealed.

16.3   What can be appealed?

If you or your spouse is unhappy with final decisions made by the judge in your case, either of you can file an appeal. Examples of decisions that can be appealed include custody, parenting time, child support, alimony, equitable distribution, and attorney fees.

16.4   Will my attorney recommend I appeal specific aspects of the final order, or will I have to request it?

Your attorney may counsel you to file an appeal on certain issues of your case; you may also ask your lawyer whether there is a legitimate basis for an appeal of any decision you believe is wrong. Talk to your attorney regarding the decisions most dissatisfying to you. Your lawyer can advise which issues have the greatest likelihood of success on appeal, in light of the facts of your case and North Carolina law.

16.5   When should an appeal be filed?

An appeal should be filed only after careful consultation with your lawyer when you believe that the judge has made a serious error under the law or the facts of your case. Among the factors you and your attorney should discuss are:

- Whether the judge had authority under the law to make the decisions set forth in the judgment
- The likelihood of the success of your appeal
- The risk that an appeal by you will encourage an appeal by your former spouse
- The cost of an appeal
- The length of time an appeal can be expected to take
- The impact of a delay in the case during the appeal

The deadline for filing an appeal is thirty days from the date that a final order is entered in your case. It is important that you are clear about the deadline that applies in your case, so talk to your attorney at once if you are thinking about an appeal.

16.6 Are there any disadvantages to filing an appeal?

There can be disadvantages to filing an appeal, including:

- Uncertainty of the outcome
- Increased attorney fees and costs
- The risk of a worse outcome on appeal than you received at trial
- Delay of a final resolution
- Prolonged conflict between you and your former spouse
- The risk of a second trial occurring after the appeal
- Difficulty in obtaining closure and moving forward with your life

16.7 Is an attorney necessary to appeal?

The appeals process is very detailed and specific, with set deadlines and specific court rules. Given the complex nature of the appellate process, you should have an attorney if you intend to file an appeal.

16.8 How long does the appeals process usually take?

It depends. An appeal can take anywhere from many months to many years. An appeal may also result in the appellate court requiring further proceedings by the trial court. This will result in further delay.

16.9 What are the steps in the appeals process?

There are many steps that your lawyer will take on your behalf in the appeals process, including:

- Identifying the issues to be appealed
- Filing a notice with the court of your intent to appeal
- Obtaining the necessary court documents and trial exhibits to send to the appellate court
- Obtaining trial transcripts, a written copy of testimony by witnesses, and statements by the judge and the lawyers made in the presence of the court reporter
- Performing legal research to support your arguments on appeal

- Preparing and filing a document known as a "brief," which sets forth the facts of the case and the relevant law, complete with citations to court transcripts, court documents, and prior cases
- Making an oral argument before the judges of the appellate court

16.10 Is filing and pursuing an appeal expensive?

Yes. In addition to filing fees and attorney fees, there is likely to be a substantial cost for the preparation of the transcript of the trial testimony.

16.11 If I do not file an appeal, can I ever go back to court to change my final order?

Certain aspects of final orders are not modifiable, such as the division of property and debts or the award of attorney fees. Other parts of your final order, such as support or matters regarding the children, may be modified if there has been a substantial and material change in circumstances. A modification of custody or parenting time for minor children will also require you to show that the change would be in their best interest. If you believe that you have a basis for a modification of your judgment, consult with your attorney.

In Closing

In the days, and perhaps weeks, ahead, the process of divorce will come to an end. Now pause and breathe. Acknowledge yourself for the courage you have shown in examining your unique situation, needs, and goals. Now, you are facing your future—recasting yourself into a new life. You are looking more closely at your living situation, the needs of your children, your financial security, and your personal growth and healing. You are seeing your situation and facing the truth about what you now need. You are taking action to propel yourself into new possibilities.

From here, it is time to take inventory of the lessons learned, goals met, and actions yet to take. Celebrate each of those steps forward and be gentle with yourself over the occasional misstep backward. You have transitioned through this time when everything is reduced to the core of you. Gone are the familiar habits of your marriage. With every day moving closer to the completion of your divorce, your grief will begin to subside and your energy will increase as you move toward a fresh start. All the best to you as you move forward in life's journey.

Resources

Annual Credit Report Request Service
P.O. Box 105283
Atlanta, GA 30348
Phone: (877) 322–8228
www.annualcreditreport.com

This website offers a centralized service for consumers to request annual credit reports. It was created by the three nationwide consumer credit reporting companies—Equifax, Experian, and TransUnion. AnnualCreditReport.com processes requests for free credit file disclosures (commonly called credit reports). Under the *Fair and Accurate Credit Transactions Act (FACT Act),* consumers can request and obtain a free credit report once every twelve months from each of the three nationwide consumer credit reporting companies. AnnualCreditReport.com offers consumers a fast and convenient way to request, view, and print their credit reports in a secure Internet environment. It also provides options to request reports by telephone and by mail.

Council for Children's Rights
601 East Fifth Street, Suite 510
Charlotte, NC 28202
Phone: (704) 372-7961
www.cfcrights.org

Council for Children's Rights' mission is to lead the community to stand up for every child's right to be safe, healthy, and educated. Serving the Charlotte-Mecklenburg area, the Council's lawyers and advocates provide services for children regardless of socioeconomic status and work in the areas of education, abuse and neglect, health, mental health, contested custody cases, domestic violence, and juvenile justice.

Internal Revenue Service (IRS)

www.irs.gov

Phone: (800) 829-1040 tax assistance for individual tax questions or (800) 829-4933 for business tax questions.

The IRS website allows you to search for any key word, review publications and information on tax questions, or submit a question via e-mail or phone to an IRS representative.

Legal Aid of North Carolina

www.legalaidnc.org

Phone: (866) 219-5262 (toll free)

Legal Aid of North Carolina has statewide offices providing free legal help to low-income North Carolinians in civil cases. Attorneys defend clients from violence and sexual assault and help secure and enforce protective orders for victims of domestic violence and sexual assault. Services include a self-help library and information on self-help clinics.

Legal Services of Southern Piedmont

1431 Elizabeth Avenue

Charlotte, NC 28204

Phone: Mecklenburg County Client Help Line: (704) 376-1600 outside Mecklenburg County: (800) 438-1254

www.lssp.org

Legal Services of Southern Piedmont (LSSP) provides legal assistance in civil matters to low-income persons in the Charlotte area and in west-central North Carolina.

Mecklenburg County Community Support Services —Women's Commission

Hal Marshall Services Center

700 North Tryon Street

Charlotte, NC 28202

Phone: (704) 336-3210

http://charmeck.org/Mecklenburg/county/Community SupportServices/WomensCommission

The Mecklenburg County Community Support Services Women's Commission is an advocacy organization located in the Charlotte-Mecklenburg area providing prevention and intervention services including services for adult victims and child witnesses of domestic violence. Adult programs offer individual counseling and support groups to victims of domestic violence and the children's services provide counseling, support, and education to children and youth affected by domestic violence and dating abuse in the hopes of ending the cycle of abuse.

Mecklenburg County Self-Serve Center

832 East Fourth Street, Suite 3350
Charlotte, NC 28202
Phone: (704) 686-0210
www.nccourts.org/County/Mecklenburg/selfserve

Located within the Mecklenburg County Courthouse, the Self-Serve Center contains forms and instructions to assist all community members with modification of child support; visitation, and/or child custody; child support; visitation; child custody; violation of a court order for child support; domestic violence; and instructions on how to bring a motion for visitation before the court in a child support case. The Self-Serve Center also contains forms for Absolute Divorce (Uncontested) inside the courthouse. Lawyer referral information, community resources, and a legal glossary to help understand court terminology can be found on the Self-Serve Center website.

North Carolina Central University
School of Law Family Law Clinic

http://law.nccu.edu/clinics/family-law/
Phone: Referrals are made through Legal Aid of NC-Durham at (919) 688-6396

This clinic offers free legal assistance stressing the importance of a holistic approach to the practice of family law. In addition to providing a service to the community, the clinic also trains students to identify potential social or mental health issues and address them by referring clients to appropriate community services. The clinic is staffed by law students under the supervision of the NC Central University School of Law faculty members.

North Carolina Child Support
Centralized Collections Payment Processing Center

Phone: (800) 992-9457 (toll free)
https://nc.smartchildsupport.com

This website includes specific sections for individuals receiving support, for individuals paying support, and for employers of individuals paying support. A toll-free automated system to check on the status of the receipt and disbursement of child support, as well as any outstanding balance owed, can be accessed by calling (800) 992-9457.

North Carolina Child Support Guidelines
https://nddhacts01.dhhs.state.nc.us/WorkSheet.jsp
The North Carolina Child Support Guidelines are available online along with printable work sheets for primary custody, joint shared custody, and split custody.

North Carolina Department
of Health and Human Services Child
Support Enforcement
NC Child Support Services
P.O. Box 20800
Raleigh, NC 27619-0800
Phone: (252) 789-5225, (800) 992-9457 (toll-free)
www.ncdhhs.gov/assistance/childrens-services/child-support-enforcement

North Carolina State Bar
Legal Specialization
PO Box 25908
Raleigh, NC 27611
Phone: (919) 828-4620
www.nclawspecialists.gov
The North Carolina State Bar's Legal Specialization website lists the practice areas of legals specialists, benefits, and where to find a legal specialist in your area.

Social Security Administration
Office of Public Inquiries
1100 West High Rise
Baltimore, MD 21235
Phone: (800) 772-1213
www.ssa.gov
The SSA website enables users to search for a question or word, submit questions via e-mail, or review recent publications.

Glossary

Affidavit: A written statement of facts made under oath and signed before a notary public. Affidavits are used primarily when there will not be a hearing in open court with live testimony. The attorney will prepare an affidavit to present relevant facts. Affidavits may be signed by the parties or in some cases by witnesses. The person signing the affidavit may be referred to as the *affiant.*

Alimony: Court-ordered spousal support payments from one party to another, often to enable the recipient spouse to become economically independent.

Allegation: A statement that one party claims is true.

Answer: A written response to the petition for divorce. It serves to admit or deny the allegations in the complaint and may also make claims against the opposing party. This is sometimes called a *responsive pleading.* An answer should be filed within thirty days of either (a) the complaint being served by the sheriff or (b) the defendant's voluntary appearance being filed with the court.

Appeal: The process by which a higher court reviews the decision of a lower court. In North Carolina family law cases, a person will first file an appeal with the North Carolina Court of Appeals. After that appeal is decided there may be a further appeal to the North Carolina Supreme Court.

Application for removal of jurisdiction: A parent's written request to the court seeking permission to relocate to another state with the children.

Chambers: The private room or office of a judge or any place where the judge transacts official business when not holding a session of the court.

Child support: Financial support for a child paid by the noncustodial parent to the custodial parent.

Complaint: The first document filed with the clerk of the court in an action for divorce, separation, or paternity. The complaint sets forth the facts on which the requested relief is based.

Consent order: A court order that all parties agree to.

Contempt of court: The willful and intentional failure of a party to comply with a court order, judgment, or decree. Contempt may be punishable by a fine or jail.

Contested case: Any case in which the parties cannot reach an agreement. A contested case will result in a trial to have the judge decide disputed issues.

Court order: A court-issued document setting forth the judge's orders. An order can be issued based upon the parties agreement or the judge's decision. An order may require the parties to perform certain acts or set forth their rights and responsibilities. An order is put in writing, signed by the judge, and filed with the court.

Court order acceptable for processing (COAP): A type of court order that provides for payment of civil service retirement to a former spouse.

Cross-examination: The questioning of a witness by the opposing counsel during trial or at a deposition, in response to questions asked by the other lawyer.

Custody: The legal right and responsibility awarded by a court for the possession, care of, and decision making for a minor child.

Defendant: The responding party to a divorce; the party who did not file the complaint initiating the divorce.

Deposition: A witness's testimony taken out of court, under oath, and in the presence of lawyers and a court reporter. If a person gives different testimony at the time of trial, he or she can be impeached with the deposition testimony; that is, statements made at a deposition can be used to show untruthfulness if a different answer is given at trial.

Direct examination: The initial questioning of a witness in court by the lawyer who called him or her to the stand.

Glossary

Discovery: A process used by attorneys to discover information from the opposing party for the purpose of fully assessing a case for settlement or trial. Types of discovery include interrogatories, requests for production of documents, and requests for admissions.

Divorce decree: A final court order dissolving the marriage, dividing property and debts, ordering support, and entering other orders regarding finances and the minor children.

Domestic violence: Intentionally causing bodily injury, attempting to cause bodily injury, or placing a person with whom one has had a personal relationship in fear of serious bodily injury or continued harassment. North Carolina defines a "personal relationship" as one where the parties are: current or former spouses; persons of the opposite sex who live or have lived together; persons related as parents and children or grandparents and grandchildren; persons having a child in common; current and former household members; or any persons of the opposite sex who are in a dating relationship or have been in a dating relationship.

Domestic violence protective order (DVPO): A court order restraining the defendant from further acts of domestic violence. A protective order may include awarding temporary custody of a minor child to the plaintiff.

Equitable distribution of property: The method by which real and personal property and debts are divided in a divorce. North Carolina law presumes an equal distribution of marital assets and debts is equitable but will take multiple factors into consideration in dividing marital property.

Ex parte: Usually in reference to a motion, the term used to describe an appearance of only one party before the judge, without the other party being present. For example, an *ex parte* restraining order may be granted immediately after the filing of a complaint for divorce.

Guardian *ad litem* (GAL): A person, often a lawyer or mental health professional, appointed by the court to conduct an investigation regarding the children's best interest.

Hearing: Any proceeding before the court for the purpose of resolving disputed issues between the parties through presentation of testimony, affidavits, exhibits, or argument.

Hold-harmless clause: A term in a court order that requires one party to assume responsibility for a debt and to protect the other spouse from any loss or expense in connection with it, as in "to hold harmless from liability."

In camera: A judicial proceeding in which all or part of a case is held in a judge's chambers or when all spectators are excluded from the courtroom.

Interim distribution: In the equitable distribution process, on proper motion of either party, the court may distribute to one party certain items of property prior to entering a final judgment unless good cause is shown that such a distribution should not be made.

Interrogatories: Written questions sent from one party to the other that are used to obtain facts or opinions related to the divorce.

Joint legal custody: The shared right and responsibility of both parents awarded by the court for possession, care, and decision making for children.

Joint physical custody: The shared right and responsibility of both parents awarded by the court for supervision and parenting of the child. Joint physical custody may or may not be equal and is defined by the parties in a parenting schedule or by court order.

Mediation: A process by which a neutral third party facilitates negotiations between the parties on a wide range of issues.

Motion: A written application to the court for relief, such as temporary child support, custody, or restraining orders.

Motion to modify: A party's written request to the court to change a prior order regarding custody, child support, alimony, or any other order that the court may change by law.

Notice of hearing: A written statement sent to the opposing lawyer or spouse listing the date and place of a hearing and the nature of the matters that will be heard by the court. In North Carolina, one party is required to give the other party reasonable notice of any court hearing.

Party: The person in a legal action whose rights or interests will be affected by the divorce. For example, in a divorce the parties include the husband and wife.

Pending: During the case. For example, the judge may award you temporary support while your case is pending.

Petitioner: A term formerly used to refer to the plaintiff or person who files the complaint seeking a divorce.

Glossary

Plaintiff: The person who files the complaint initiating a divorce.

Pleadings: Documents filed with the court seeking a court order.

Preliminary injunction: A temporary court order commanding or preventing an action that is issued before or during trial to prevent an irreparable injury from occurring before the court has a chance to decide the case. Preliminary injunctions will only be issued after the defendant receives notice and an opportunity to be heard.

Qualified domestic relations order (QDRO): A type of court order that provides for direct payment from a retirement account to a former spouse.

Qualified medical support order (QMSO): A type of court order that provides a former spouse certain rights regarding medical insurance and information.

Request for production of documents: A written request for documents sent from one party to the other during the discovery process.

Sequester: To order prospective witnesses out of the courtroom until they have concluded giving their testimony.

Setoff: A debt or financial obligation of one spouse that is deducted from the debt or financial obligation of the other spouse.

Settlement: The agreed resolution of disputed issues.

Show cause: Written application to the court to hold another person in contempt of court for violating or failing to comply with a current court order.

Stipulation: An agreement reached between parties or an agreement by their attorneys.

Subpoena: A document delivered to a person or witness that requires him or her to appear in court, appear for a deposition, or produce documents. Failure to comply could result in punishment by the court. A subpoena requesting documents is called a subpoena *duces tecum.*

Temporary restraining order: An order of the court prohibiting a party from certain behavior. For example, a temporary restraining order may order a person not to transfer any funds during a pending divorce action.

Trial: A formal court hearing in which the judge will decide disputed issues raised by the party's pleadings.

Uncontested divorce: The type of divorce North Carolina has in which the court does not require evidence of marital misconduct. This means that abandonment, cruelty, and adultery are neither relevant nor required to be proven for the purposes of granting the divorce.

Under advisement: A term used to describe the status of a case, usually after a court hearing on a motion or a trial, when the judge has not yet made a decision.

Index

207

Index

112
witnesses, 86
domestic violence, 10, 79
domestic violence protection
orders (DVPO), 15, 85, 87,
88
drug abuse, 81, 86, 91, 101,
108, 110, 113, 138, 151

E

early neutral evaluation, 79,
83
earning capacity, 124, 136
education history, 66, 67, 124,
136, 137
embryos, 158
emergency situations, 15,
84–91
emotional abuse, 86
engagement ring, 156
equitable distribution, 2, 11,
142, 143, 157, 192
exceptions, 143
equity in business, 151
equity in home, 147
division, 147
evidence, 58, 187
admissible, 62, 66
ex parte court order, 15, 87
ex parte hearing, 87
excessive litigation, 114
exchange date for personal
property, 19
exhibits, 39
expense information, 122
expense reduction, 55–57
expert witnesses, 51, 55, 64,
69
expert-witness fees, 51, 52
extramarital relationships,
102
see also adultery, affairs
extraordinary expenses, 18

F

Fair Credit Reporting Act, 167
fair market values, 143, 146
family courts, 79
family financial settlement
program mediation, 79, 81,

82
choosing mediator, 83
fees and costs, 83
nonfinancial matters, 82
family heirlooms, 145
family history, 66
family law, 2, 33, 34
family law specialist, 33
family member or friend, 30,
33, 38, 47, 49, 55, 86, 104,
182, 187, 188
father and mother property, or
documentation, 12
fee advance, 48
fee agreements, 48, 50, 53
file stamped documents, 12
filing fees, 51
filing status for taxes, 20
final hearings, 181
final statement of decision, 7
finality of divorce decree, 21
finance charges, 167
financial accounts, 3, 4, 5,
150
financial affidavit, 65, 122,
129
financial agreements, 155
financial analyses, 39
financial disclosure statements, 5, 129
financial experts, 39
financial hardships, 179
firearms or weapons, 111,
112
fitness of parent, 119
flat fees, 28, 45, 47, 51
formal discovery, 59
types, 59
former name restoration, 20,
22
free legal advice, 44, 49
frozen embryos, 158

G

gambling problems, 151, 168
garnishment of wages, 130
gay marriage, 103
get cooperation clause, 157
gifts and inheritances, 143,

Index

Index

Index

William C. Trosch   Eric C. Trosch

About the Authors

William C. "Bill" Trosch, Esq., heads the litigation department and is the managing partner at Conrad Trosch & Kemmy, P.A., in Charlotte, North Carolina. Since 1993, he has maintained a diverse law practice with an aim toward resolving conflicts. Bill has handled a number of high-profile cases, both locally and nationally. These well-publicized cases ranged from lawsuits against the City of Charlotte to a high-profile negotiation with the N.C.A.A.

Bill is an honors graduate from the University of North Carolina at Chapel Hill; he holds degrees in economics and mathematics. He also was an honors graduate of the University of North Carolina School of Law at Chapel Hill, where he was a staff member of the *North Carolina Law Review*. His published work in the *Law Review* has been cited by many publications and courts, including the Ohio Supreme Court.

Bill also is a highly sought-after educator. He was an associate member of the graduate faculty of the University of North Carolina in Charlotte, and he taught a negotiations class for the M.B.A. program at the Belk College of Business. Bill has taught groups of lawyers and nonlawyers alike on a wide variety of legal topics for local, state, and national organizations.

A Charlotte native and a graduate of West Charlotte High School, Bill is the third generation of attorneys to practice in his family's law firm. He lives in the Cotswold area of Charlotte with his wife, Lisa, and children, Liam, Kenzie, and Gavin.

Bill can be reached through his website:
www.CTKLawyers.com

Eric C. Trosch, Esq., is certified as a legal specialist in family law by the North Carolina State Bar Board of Legal Specialization. Eric has practiced family law in North Carolina since 2002 and is now a partner at Conrad Trosch & Kemmy, P.A., heading up the Family Law Division. Eric utilizes a common-sense approach to family law and a wide array of tools to obtain the best results for his clients.

Eric received his undergraduate degree from the University of North Carolina at Chapel Hill. He earned his law degree from Wake Forest University in Winston-Salem, North Carolina, where he was the first recipient of the North Carolina Chapter of the American Academy of Matrimonial Lawyers Award for the Student Advancement of Matrimonial Law.

After graduating from law school, Eric continued his leadership in the Charlotte community. He recently completed his term as co-chair of the Mecklenburg Collaborative Law Group. He served on the North Carolina State Bar Association Family Law Council, and is also a member of the Domestic Court Committee of the Mecklenburg County Courts and the Local Rules Committee.

Eric has been recognized for his family law practice as one of the Top 100 Family Lawyers in North Carolina by the American Society of Legal Advocates. He was also named one of the Top 10 Family Law Attorneys in North Carolina under the age of forty by the National Academy of Family Law Attorneys, and was also selected as a "Rising Star in North Carolina" by *Super Lawyers*. His peers and colleagues have also highly rated his skills; he was endorsed as "Legal Elite" by Business North Carolina and recognized in "People on the Move" by the *Charlotte Business Journal*.

Eric and his wife, Elizabeth, have two children, Alec and Joseph. Eric can be reached through his website: **www.CTKLawyers.com**

Divorce Titles from Addicus Books

Visit our online catalog at www.AddicusBooks.com

Divorce in Alabama: The Legal Process, Your Rights, and What to Expect $21.95

Divorce in Arizona: The Legal Process, Your Rights, and What to Expect. $21.95

Divorce in California: The Legal Process, Your Rights, and What to Expect $21.95

Divorce in Connecticut: The Legal Process, Your Rights, and What to Expect $21.95

Divorce in Florida: The Legal Process, Your Rights, and What to Expect $21.95

Divorce in Georgia: Simple Answers to Your Legal Questions $21.95

Divorce in Hawaii: The Legal Process, Your Rights, and What to Expect $21.95

Divorce in Illinois: The Legal Process, Your Rights, and What to Expect $21.95

Divorce in Kansas: The Legal Process, Your Rights, and What to Expect $21.95

Divorce in Louisiana: The Legal Process, Your Rights, and What to Expect $21.95

Divorce in Maine: The Legal Process, Your Rights, and What to Expect $21.95

Divorce in Maryland: The Legal Process, Your Rights, and What to Expect $21.95

Divorce in Michigan: The Legal Process, Your Rights, and What to Expect. $21.95

Divorce in Mississippi: The Legal Process, Your Rights, and What to Expect. $21.95

Divorce in Missouri: The Legal Process, Your Rights, and What to Expect $21.95

Divorce in Nebraska: The Legal Process, Your Rights, and What to Expect—2nd Edition $21.95

Divorce in Nevada: The Legal Process, Your Rights, and What to Expect. $21.95

Divorce in New Jersey: The Legal Process, Your Rights, and What to Expect $21.95

Divorce in New York: The Legal Process, Your Rights, and What to Expect $21.95

Divorce in North Carolina: Answers to Your Legal Questions. $21.95

Divorce in Oklahoma: The Legal Process, Your Rights, and What to Expect $21.95

Divorce in Tennessee: The Legal Process, Your Rights, and What to Expect $21.95

Divorce in Virginia: The Legal Process, Your Rights, and What to Expect $21.95

Divorce in Washington: The Legal Process, Your Rights, and What to Expect $21.95

Divorce in West Virginia: The Legal Process, Your Rights, and What to Expect $21.95

Divorce in Wisconsin: The Legal Process, Your Rights, and What to Expect $21.95

Daily Meditations for Healing from Divorce: Discovering the New You. $21.95

To Order Books:
Visit us online at: www.AddicusBooks.com
Call toll free: (800) 888-4741

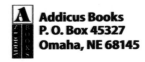

Addicus Books
P. O. Box 45327
Omaha, NE 68145

To order books from Addicus Books:

Please send:

_____copies of_____
                                    (Title of book)
        at $ _____each   TOTAL   _____
        NE residents add 5% sales tax   _____

        Shipping/Handling
            $6.75 for first book
            $1.10 for each additional book   _____

                TOTAL ENCLOSED   _____

Name _____
Address _____
City _____State_____Zip _____

        ☐ Visa   ☐ Mastercard   ☐ AMEX   ☐ Discover
Credit card number _____
Expiration date _____
Three-digit CVV number on back of card _____

Order by credit card or personal check.

To Order Books:
Visit us online at: www.AddicusBooks.com
Call toll free: (800) 888-4741

Addicus Books
P. O. Box 45327
Omaha, NE 68145